An Insider's History of the Swingin' Medallions

An Insider's History of the Swingin' Medallions

Carroll Bledsoe

Copyright © 2018 by Carroll Bledsoe.

Library of Congress Control Number: 2018907562
ISBN: Hardcover 978-1-9845-3701-0
　　　 Softcover 978-1-9845-3700-3
　　　 eBook 978-1-9845-3699-0

All rights reserved. No part of this book may be reproduced or transmitted in any form or by any means, electronic or mechanical, including photocopying, recording, or by any information storage and retrieval system, without permission in writing from the copyright owner.

Any people depicted in stock imagery provided by Getty Images are models, and such images are being used for illustrative purposes only.
Certain stock imagery © Getty Images.

Print information available on the last page.

Rev. date: 06/27/2018

To order additional copies of this book, contact:
Xlibris
1-888-795-4274
www.Xlibris.com
Orders@Xlibris.com
774932

THIS BOOK IS dedicated to John McElrath—Mr. Medallion. Without his tireless and lifelong dedication to the group and passion for music, none of this story would have taken place. He took all of us along with him for the ride. Over fifty years of doing anything is remarkable. Over fifty years of existing as a band is unheard of. John is the one to thank for this incredible lifelong journey.

CONTENTS

Foreword ix
Preface xiii

Chapter 1   My Love of Music Begins 1
Chapter 2   What? Me Sing? Are You Kidding? 5
Chapter 3   The Discords 8
Chapter 4   Panama City Beach, Here We Come 13
Chapter 5   Birmingham or Bust! 19
Chapter 6   1966—Double Shot Goes National 25
Chapter 7   Double Shot Tour Begins 30
Chapter 8   California, Here We Come 33
Chapter 9   Oregon and Washington 37
Chapter 10 Atlanta, Georgia, Y'all 39
Chapter 11 East Coast Tour Begins 41
Chapter 12 We Love You, Too, Pittsburgh 43
Chapter 13 New York, New York 44
Chapter 14 Buses, Planes, and Automobiles 46
Chapter 15 Welcome Home 49
Chapter 16 Aloha! 51
Chapter 17 A Battle of Accents 54
Chapter 18 Mondo Daytona 57
Chapter 19 Don't Worry, Jesse, We Will Get You Out 59
Chapter 20 The Wreck 61
Chapter 21 LSU 63
Chapter 22 Return to Myrtle Beach 65
Chapter 23 Friends Along the Way 67
Chapter 24 Jekyll Island—2006 70
Chapter 25 Tooting Our Own Horns 72
Chapter 26 Chicken Man 75

Chapter 27	Memories	79
Chapter 28	In Loving Memory	82
Chapter 29	The Party on the Mountain—Fifty Years!	87
Chapter 30	Still Swingin'	91
Chapter 31	Post Script	95
Acknowledgments		101

FOREWORD

FOREWORD
By: "Rocking" Dave Roddy

AS A DISC jockey on WSGN in Birmingham, Alabama, I enjoyed the benefits of a strong relationship with youth and, as a result, parlayed the station's popularity as a concert promoter.

In the spring of l964, there was talk of a great new band that was performing at the Old Hickory Beach Club in Panama City, Florida. One after the other, in-the-know teens encouraged me to bring the Swingin' Medallions to Birmingham. Local fraternities and sororities had been unable to hire the group due to a contractual stipulation that permitted the Medallions only one day off a week.

Undaunted, I drove to Florida to see what the buzz was all about. My young talent scouts were right on the money! The Swingin' Medallions' big horn sound and high-energy choreography absolutely blew me away.

Their exciting show would be unleashed in Birmingham only if we could find a way to work around their contractual obligation. This was a pretty tall order since the group's only day off was Monday ... the worst day of the week to promote a concert, right?

Well, maybe not! We'd call it "Medallion Monday" and do it *every* Monday all summer long! Based on WSGN's dominance with youth and the group's burgeoning popularity, founder John McElrath agreed for them to come to Birmingham on a joint venture, but the odds were pretty good. We started out at a country club for an afternoon pool party. You know ... throw a little sand around and try to create the beach atmosphere. Nearby residents complained about loud music and crowds, so we had to move to another venue where sound wouldn't be an issue.

Nighttime was the right time for Medallion Monday, and the Swingin' Medallions began to pack the house each week, rain or shine! The hops were stand-up concerts. A few couples danced, but most people just crowded around the stage, swaying to the beat, hands in the air, singing along: "Hey-hey-aye-baby, I wanna know-oh-oh if you'll be my girl."

The young, talented, hard-working guys from South Carolina earned more in one day in Birmingham than they made all week in Panama City! They loved the Magic City, and we loved them. Weekly turnouts grew so much that we had to move to a new auditorium, doubling our capacity and parking.

We regularly maxed out legal crowd limits. When the limits were met, people in line were permitted to enter only when someone exited, causing future lines to form several hours before shows began. Nobody wanted to miss a single minute of the Swingin' Medallions' show!

The next year, John McElrath did not renew the Old Hickory contract, and Saturday nights opened up. For several summers, the Medallions appeared twice a week and continued to pack 'em in every time. It was truly amazing. I don't think any nationally known group could have drawn a more consistently huge crowd.

In summer of 1965, "Double Shot" became number one on the charts in Birmingham, and we had to do two separate shows in order to accommodate the multitudes that flocked to get in.

Disc jockeys all across the nation heard what was happening in Birmingham and started playing their record.

Initially established as a hit in Birmingham in 1965, "Double Shot" finally started climbing *Billboard's* Top 100 a year later, where it remained on the national survey for thirteen weeks, achieving top twenty status. To have been out front with it first remains one of my proudest accomplishments as a disk jockey.

Our youthful joint venture lasted through the sixties, when I left Birmingham to open an ad agency in Columbia, South Carolina, which has kept me geographically closer to the group through the years. I truly miss the original members who have passed.

I recently enjoyed celebrating the group's fiftieth anniversary of "Double Shot" with both the surviving and current members. I am grateful for their continued friendship.

It was an amazing run for the original members, and the young guys led by John McElrath's sons Shawn and Shane are keeping it going strong. Original member Jimmy Perkins is still performing. Go see them; it's the same as always.

"One night a week is a-plenty enough; it's a good thing for me they don't bottle that stuff."

I know you will enjoy the following chronicle of the Swingin' Medallions' incredible journey, shared by original member, Carroll Bledsoe.

—Dave "Rockin'" Roddy, WSGN, Birmingham, Alabama, 1961–72

PREFACE

THIS IS THE story of eight young guys, born in small town America, who become a national sensation in the music world. In 1966, the Swingin' Medallions and their song "Double Shot of My Baby's Love" hit the charts and changed their lives forever. The band is still playing today, marking over fifty years of music. The "party band of the South" is still partying!

This *all* happened as a result of a lot of hard work, an awful lot of luck, and the strong support of family and friends.

Naturally, a lot of the recollections in this book are my own, but I also received a lot of input from other band members, both past and present. We would also like to thank everyone who helped and supported us on our journey.

Our thanks go out to Clayto Roberts and Norman Outzs. They owned the only music store in Greenwood, and they were staunch supporters of all of our records. They spent their own money running ads in the *Index-Journal*, Greenwood's local newspaper.

Our special thanks go out to all of the radio stations and deejays across the country, without whose support this would all have been impossible. We will get into more specifics on these in the book.

Thanks to all of the promoters who believed in us. Thanks to our agents, and of course, thanks to all of our fans who have supported us over the years, many for over fifty years.

Thanks for all the friends that we have made along the way. Meeting people from all across the country is a very special thing.

Now, let the party begin!

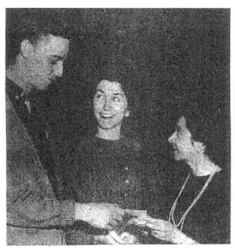

Band Members Selling Concert Tickets

Miss Frances Sterghos, left, buys a ticket for the Furman University Band concert to be presented in the Greenwood High School auditorium beginning at 8 p. m. tomorrow. Concert tickets are being sold by members of the Greenwood High band and Miss Sterghos is buying hers from Carroll Bledsoe, left, and Dale Byrd. Ticket prices are $1 for adults and 50 cents for students. All proceeds will go to the high school band. (Index-Journal Photo by Bodie McDowell).

High School Band Sells Tickets. Check out the
prices in the article.

CHAPTER 1

My Love of Music Begins

MY LOVE OF music began in high school. I was in the Greenwood High School band all four years I was in school there. I started out playing the trumpet. My junior and senior years, I switched to playing drums in the marching band and French horn in the concert band.

I fell in love with beach music my junior year in high school. A group of us guys would go to Myrtle Beach, South Carolina, the first week in June as soon as school was out for the summer.

Sonny's Pavilion at Cherry Grove Beach, the Pavilion at Pawley's Island, and the Pad at Ocean Drive Beach were the most popular places to go. There was also a club in downtown Myrtle Beach where a little-known band at the time began their career. That band was Alabama, and that club was the Bowery.

Each night we put on our official beach uniforms: a brightly colored madras shirt, white pants, Bass weejuns (penny loafers), and *no socks*! All of these places had a jukebox filled with songs by the Drifters, the Clovers, the Coasters and many more beach music hits.

We learned how to shag, which later became the state dance of South Carolina. The shag is an offspring of the jive but at a slower tempo. The dance has a basic step, and the dancers add their own variations, turns, and moves off of the basic steps such as the boogie walk and belly roll.

My favorite venue was Sonny's Pavilion. They had a large dance floor, a great selection of music on the jukebox, and they always had large crowds, which meant plenty of teenage girls to dance with.

Most of the crowd was from South Carolina, North Carolina, Virginia, and Tennessee. Of course, there were some Yankees, but they didn't know about or understand the shag. We had a ball dancing to "Sixty-Minute Man," "Zing Went the Strings of My Heart," and almost anything by the Drifters.

Most of the teenagers and college kids were around Cherry Grove Beach, Ocean Drive Beach, and Crescent Beach. All of these are located up Highway 17, a few miles north of Myrtle Beach. Today, this entire area is known simply as North Myrtle Beach. Two times a year, they celebrate SOS week. SOS used to stand for "shagging on the sand." Shaggers from back in the day pack this area to try to relive their youth.

The Pavilion at Myrtle Beach was a popular place for families and younger kids. They had an arcade, a roller coaster, and other kid rides.

Three Sets Of Winners

Winners of last night's Civitan Club talent show were the "Four Notes" composed of first row, left to right, Carroll Bledsoe, Larry Vaughn, Betty Babb and Conolly Burgess. The three boys in the group wear white shirts with a black note on the left side. Second place went to the Mockettes on the second row. They are, left to right, Peggy Kirby, Jackie Patrick, Dottie Clayton, Irene Martin, Elizabeth Ann Faulkner and Alison Marshall. Clyde Adams, in center of second row, placed third. (Index-Journal Photo by Jim Allen).

Civitans Hold Talent Contest

Four Greenwood High students, blended pleasant voices and the notes of bongo drums and a uke last night to win first place in the annual Civitan Club talent contest.

The talented group performs under the name "The Four Notes." The "Four Notes" are Betty Babb, Carroll Bledsoe, Conolly Burgess and Larry Vaughn. Civitan President Al Clark presented the group with a $20 first prize, and informed them they would have the opportunity to appear on the Sundowners television show in Augusta next Wednesday evening.

Last night's talent show was followed by an hour-long musical show by the Sundowners, a western music group from Augusta.

A $10 second prize was awarded to the Mockettes, another Greenwood High singing group. The group is composed of Irene Martin, Peggy Kirby, Elizabeth Ann Faulkner, Alison Marshall, Dottie Jo Clayton, and Jackie Patrick.

Clyde Adams won the $5 third prize. Adams strummed a guitar and sang "Into the Night" to place behind the two vocal groups.

Other contestants were David Capelle and Pam Bowie, duet; Sally Shaw, tap routine; David Capelle, solo; Pam Bowie, solo; Brenda Klugh, dance routine; Nancy Carroll Beaty, ballet number; Susan and Peggy Riddle, duet; Sylvia Foster, solo; Felicia Lawton, solo; Caroline Monroe, tap routine; Eva Culbertson, solo; Millie Blackwell, tap routine, and Margaret L. Tietin, solo.

"The Four Notes" win Talent Contest

CHAPTER 2

What? Me Sing? Are You Kidding?

IN HIGH SCHOOL, four of us formed a singing group, three boys and a girl. Betty Babb, daughter of legendary and Hall of Fame football coach Pinky Babb was the female member. She and Larry Vaughn and Conolly Burgess, two of my best friends, and I became the Four Notes. I played the baritone ukulele to accompany us.

After every Greenwood High home football game, there was a dance at the local recreation center. There would be a live band playing. Maurice Williams and the Zodiacs from Charlotte, North Carolina, were fan favorites. They sang their hits "Little Darling" and "Stay." We would perform during their intermission breaks.

Our highlight performance came when we were invited to play an assembly program at Erskine College in Due West, South Carolina. A forty-five-minute program was something we had never done before. We opened the show with a song called "Lollipop." When we finished the song, we threw lollipops into the audience. We had them hidden behind our backs. The students went wild, and we had them literally eating out of our hands the rest of the show.

I recently saw a 1958 copy of the Ninety Six newspaper that had a picture of the Four Notes on the front page. We had won first place in a talent contest there in Ninety Six. The prize was a whopping ten dollars, two dollars and fifty cents each—my first paycheck as a musician. I guess that meant we were now considered professionals.

We followed this up with a win in another talent contest. This one was sponsored by the Greenwood Civitan Club. Club president Al Clark presented us with a check for twenty dollars. We had now doubled our income to five dollars. Along with all of this money, we were given the opportunity to appear on Channel 12, WRDW, in Augusta, Georgia, on the *Sundowners Television Show*. The Sundowners were a country band from Augusta, Georgia.

"Won't You Be My Valentine?"

Students were honored with singing telegrams for Valentine Day this morning at Greenwood High School. National Honor Society members sold the telegrams through their Valentine Post Office for 15 cents and then had teams of singers deliver them. Serenading Sara Mauldin, seated, with her singing valentine are, left to right, Larry Vaughn, Carroll Bledsoe, Betty Babb and Conolly Burgess.

We had finally made it to television land. We also appeared on the Carroll Sexton Show at WCRS, 1450 on the AM dial in Greenwood. Carroll was a celebrity in his own right in Greenwood, and he hosted a local show on the station every weekday morning. Later on, Chuck Sexton, his son, would be one of my best algebra students. He also played on a recreation department basketball team that I coached. We won the state championship.

The Medallions In Action

From Left to Right: Jimmy Roark, Bobby Crowder, Joe Morris, Larry Roark, Carroll Bledsoe, John McElrath and Dwight Styron.

Organized for only a year, the "Medallions" are now widely acclaimed in Sought Carolina. They are pictured here performing for Lander College for the 1963 Rat Hop. Carroll Bledsoe is a Lander Graduate and Joe Morris and John McElrath are both undergrads, giving Lander a rightful claim to the Medallions.

CHAPTER 3

The Discords

AFTER HIGH SCHOOL graduation, I enrolled at Lander College, now Lander University, in Greenwood. In those days, Lander was primarily a women's college. Men were admitted only as day students. We were not permitted to live on campus in the dorms. Darn! But the ratio of over four hundred females to seventy-five males more than made up for that little inconvenience.

I received a letter from Katy Hollingsworth, who was the dean of students. It was addressed to "Miss" Carroll Bledsoe, and it asked me to list my top three choices for a roommate. After I stopped laughing, I called the school. I told them that I trusted their judgement and anyone they picked would be fine with me. Needless to say, that never happened, but it still gives me a chuckle after all these years.

Lander was a small school. Everyone knew everyone. When we were not in class, we spent a lot of time in the student center. We played a lot of Ping-Pong there.

While at Lander, I became close friends with John McElrath, the founder of the Swingin' Medallions, and with Jerry Lazenby. John was from Ninety Six, South Carolina. Jerry was originally from Birmingham, Alabama but had moved to Greenwood. He now lives in Austin, Texas. John played football and basketball in high school, and he was a talented musician.

We met Freddy Bailey from Ware Shoals, South Carolina, and we formed a singing group called the Discords. We performed at school and around town. We even played once for the Ware Shoals National Guard for an oyster stew supper thanks to Freddy. Had we hit the big time? John and I both played baritone ukuleles to provide the accompaniment.

Around 1962, John and Joe Morris, also of Ninety Six, South Carolina, decided to form a band. John and Joe would hang out with John's cousins, Larry and Jimmy Roark, in John's yard in Ninety Six. In the summer, you could hear music coming from the open windows of a local beer joint. Blues and soul music could be heard by Jimmy Reed, Little Milton, and other great blues artists. The guys were intrigued by the music, and they decided that's what they wanted to do. Bobby Crowder, Dwight Styron, and John Hancock, along with Larry and Jimmy Roark, were among the first members of the group. John played keyboard, and Joe played drums. They were called the Medallions. They found out later that there was already a band called the Medallions, so they changed their name to the Swingin' Medallions.

John contacted me and invited me to join the group on trumpet and vocals. John also met Gary "Cubby" Culbertson, who had moved to Greenwood as the manager of the Case Piano music store. Cubby had played with a group in Columbia called the Travelers. Cubby was a great guitar player, a real showman, and a comedian. He also excelled on keyboard.

At this time, we practiced in Ninety Six at Smokey Joe's Cafe. We set up in a back banquet room. While in Columbia, Cubby had heard a group called Dick Holler and the Holidays perform at the Army-Navy club there. One day Joe heard Cubby playing a song and asked him what it was.

The song had been put out on a local record label in Columbia. Cubby wrote down the words to the song on a napkin, and we worked up our version of "Double Shot of My Baby's Love." This became our first big break. John worked up a distinctive organ intro on his Farfisa organ and played the bass on his electric Wurlitzer piano.

In 1964, the Vietnam War was in the wings. Cubby was in the Army Reserves. He had to bow out of the group. Perrin Gleaton, a guitar player from Clemson, South Carolina, took his place. He was another great, smooth guitar player and also a great guy who fit in with the group immediately.

We regularly played a club in Greenwood called the Round Table. Fraternity boys from Athens and Columbia came to town every week to date Lander girls. This gave us a connection to play fraternity parties in South Carolina and Georgia. We must have played every fraternity at the University of Georgia. You could say that this was our second lucky break.

From Left to Right: Joe Morris, Perrin Gleaton, Brent Fortson, Carroll Bledsoe, John McElrath and Steve Caldwell

Summer of 1964, Panama City Beach, Florida.

CHAPTER 4

Panama City Beach, Here We Come

STEVE CALDWELL AND Brent Fortson, both of Greenwood, had now joined the group on saxophone. Brent had played in a local group, the Little Rebels. He was still in high school. Steve and Brent both worked hard at learning all about the saxophone.

Steve's father, Earl Caldwell, purchased the Old Hickory, a barbeque restaurant on the beach in Panama City, Florida. He booked us for the entire summer. The club had a patio right on the beach, and this is where we practiced in the afternoons. We usually attracted a crowd of beachgoers, and this is how we advertised.

I was teaching algebra at Northside Junior High School in Greenwood. Everyone else was still in school, so we all had the same summer break. We played six nights a week and had Monday nights off.

We added Rick Godwin of Columbia on trumpet and Freddie Pugh of Columbia on saxophone. We now had two trumpets and three saxophones for a big, big brass sound. This was perfect for soul music and the Motown sound. All of the English groups and groups like the James Gang were without horns—just guitars. This was our sound.

Panama City Beach is the summer destination for the college crowd from Georgia, Florida, Louisiana, Mississippi, and Alabama—especially Alabama. We met people from all over the southeast and from numerous universities. All of this opened more doors to get fraternity party gigs at Auburn, Alabama, Georgia Tech, LSU, Vanderbilt, Tennessee, and Georgia—especially Georgia.

We later learned that one of the fraternities we played for at Georgia had a member who would later become a famous author, columnist, and comedian—Lewis Grizzard.

He even mentioned us in his book *Elvis Is Dead and I Don't Feel So Good Myself.* To quote Lewis: "A few white bands were still in vogue as well. The most notable of which were the Swingin' Medallions. They sang 'Double Shot of My Baby's Love,' and even now when I hear that song, I makes me want to stand outside in the hot sun with a milkshake cup full of beer in one hand and a slightly drenched nineteen year old coed in the other."[1]

Later on, the band would play for one of his birthday parties. I had all of his books and even saw his comedy show in Spartanburg, South Carolina, years later.

Joe Morris picked up Perrin Gleaton in Columbia for the trip to Florida. Joe had a small MG convertible. He had to pack for the whole summer, so his car was loaded down. Perrin had about the same amount of luggage. They had to tie bags on the trunk of the car. The worst part was Perrin's guitar and case. He had to stand it on end on the floorboard between his legs for the entire trip. Agony!

The Old Hickory was originally a barbecue restaurant. Earl Caldwell—the owner and Steve's father—had renovated it to be used as a nightclub. The only advertising that he had done was to place a small white sign out front that said Live Band Tonight.

We had to go to work. The next morning we went to a local drugstore and bought out their entire inventory of poster paper, craft paper, and magic markers. We made posters and delivered them to every motel on the strip. We also bought a roll of raffle tickets. We walked the entire beach handing out flyers and the tickets for one free admission to the club. This worked great, and we had a large crowd that first night. It also endeared us to the locals.

---

[1] 1 Grizzard, Lewis. Elvis Is Dead and I Don't Feel So Good Myself, pg. 57. Peachtree Publishing, LTD, Atalnta, GA, 1984

From Left to Right: Freddie Pugh, Carroll Bledsoe, John McElrath, Joe Morris, Steve Caldwell, Perrin Gleaton, and Brent Fortson.

A hot Saturday afternoon matinee at the Old Hickory in Panama City, Florida.

The beach had an army of lifeguards. We admitted them every night for free. They really spread the word.

The crowds in Panama City got so large that we had to start having a matinee show on Saturday and Sunday afternoons. People would pack the place, standing on tables to get a better view of the band. Many days they completely blocked out the sun.

It was not all work that summer. John and I played a lot of golf. We rode the local roller coaster and visited a lot of great restaurants.

Since we were at the ocean, some of us decided to go deep sea fishing. The boat left the dock at 3:00 a.m., so we had to hurry after we finished at 2:00 a.m. We did this only twice. The first trip was terrific! The boat would take us out seventy-five miles. They had bunk beds below deck, so we could sleep for a while. The weather was beautiful, and the sea was calm. We caught red snapper and grouper mostly. When we returned to the dock, people were there to buy the fish—seventy-five cents per pound for the red snapper and forty cents per pound for the grouper. We had to use electric reels because the water was so deep. We caught a lot of fish. We made more money than the trip had cost us.

An interesting side note: Using the electric reel, the groupers would come up so fast that they would get the bends. The tongue would swell up to the size of a baseball bat handle. Very freaky looking!

The second trip was a complete opposite of the first. On the trip out, the water was choppy. When we arrived at our location at dawn, it had become stormy. At one point the captain spotted a water spout (a tornado over the ocean) on the horizon. We headed back to shore. No one complained because we spent most of the day below deck in our bunks. Can you say seasick? That was our last fishing trip.

The Old Dutch Club down the street was our main competition. The James Gang was their most popular band. If we were sold out, our overflow would go there. The club had been there several years, and the people did like the place, but we ruled Panama City in 1964 and 1965.

Remember the song "Louie Louie" by the Kingsmen? They played once at the Old Dutch. Joe met their drummer one day and had a long conversation with him. Joe got the words to the song. He is one of a small group of people who know all of the words to that song. They were purposely slurred on the record.

It was a lot of hard work, but we loved it. Singing six nights a week can take its toll until you get used to it. I became hoarse and actually developed callouses on my vocal cords. I was told to rest them as much as possible—no talking or singing. I think the other guys enjoyed the no talking part.

May 1966 Double Shot #1 in Birmingham! We outsold the Beatles, Elvis, and everyone else! Our heartfelt thanks go out to WSGN Raido and their dee jay, Dave Ruddle, A. K. A. Rocking Dave Roddy. We can never thank him enough.

CHAPTER 5

Birthmingham or Bust!

DURING THE SUMMER of 1964, we met people from all over Alabama—Dothan, Enterprise, Opelika, and Birmingham. We began a new tradition. When we finished playing Sunday night at 2:00 a.m., we packed up and drove six hours to Birmingham. I had a little Corvair, and Joe had an MG sports car. We had a friendly little competition as to who would get there first. Joe would take off and lead, but the little Corvair plugged along like the tortoise. Joe must have made several stops because we always got there first.

In 1964, Duke Rumore was a deejay at a radio station in Birmingham. He held dances at the Legion Field Armory on Monday nights. He also put on several matinees at the Cascade Plunge, a swimming complex in Birmingham.

We alternated Monday nights playing for Rocking Dave Roddy (whose real name was Dave Ruddle) of WSGN radio. Dave held his dances at the Oporto Armory on the east side of town. We continued this for the entire summer. In 1965, we played exclusively for Dave Roddy. At that time, things began to take off for us. In Birmingham, our weekly appearance was affectionately known as Medallion Monday. The crowds grew and grew, and we had to start doing two shows a night: Run one crowd out, run a second crowd in.

A large group of regulars came every single week. We were afraid that they might get tired of the same old thing every week. We decided that we needed to try some different things to keep that from happening. That's when we decided to add some new wrinkles to our show and mix it up a little.

We normally wore Swingin' Medallion shirts and white jeans. One week we did a show dressed as hippies, complete with loud, flowery shirts and leather vests with tassels. The crowd loved it!

Front Row Left to Right: Freddie Pugh, Joe Morris, and John McElrath
Back Row Left to Right: Carroll Bledsoe, Perrin Gleaton, Rick Godwin, Brent Fortson and Steve Caldwell.

The Medallion from 1964.

From Left to Right: Dave Roddy, Joe Morris, Brent Fortson Freddie Pugh, John McElrath, Carroll Bledsoe, Steve Caldwell, Perrin Gleaton and Rick Godwin.

Partying at the Country Club Pool

The biggest hit was the night we had a whipped cream fight. For our second set, we came out dressed in tuxedos. Joe Morris came out from behind his drums to sing "Long Tall Texan." Charlie Webber (trumpet and vocals) and Jimbo Door (guitar and vocals) had replaced Freddie Pugh and Perrin Gleaton for this summer's run. During Joe's song, Charlie snuck up behind Joe and hit him in the face with a cream pie. We all had cans of Reddi-Wip and went at it. We sprayed each other and a good portion of the crowd down front. The crowd went crazy! But we learned a valuable lesson: Whipped cream sours, and it can get down inside a microphone stand. That odor lasted for days! We never tried that again.

Birmingham became like a second home for us. We had a large and loyal following in the city. A large group of loyal fans showed up every time they opened the doors. Johnny Cox, who came along a little later, married a girl from Birmingham. She was one of the regulars. Birmingham will always hold a special place in our hearts alongside Panama City.

Years later, I went camping with friends in Panama City and almost didn't recognize the place. Boy, had it grown! It still has the most beautiful beaches and the whitest sand in the world.

I met my first wife while attending Lander: Melody Long, from Asheville, North Carolina. She was a year behind me in school. We started dating my junior year. After she graduated, we got married, and she came with me to Panama City for the summer. We later had three beautiful daughters—Cindy, Kelly, and Wendy.

We were married for seven years before tragedy struck. Shortly after the third child was born, Melody went into a deep depression. Her parents, my parents, her doctors, and I tried everything possible to snap her out of it. Her mother came to visit to help out, but while she was visiting Melody took her own life. It was the hardest thing I have ever had to go through.

Postpartum depression is an awful condition to endure. Thanks to family, friends, and the guys in the band, I got through it, but it took time. Melody's mother, Nell Lee Long, was very supportive of me and did everything she could to help. We remained close, and later on in life the girls moved to St. Simons Island, Georgia, to live with her for a while. She lived there until she died in her mid-ninetys. She would still put on her bathing suit and go to the beach every week.

This was an ad placed in the local newspaper promoting our first album. Clayto Roberts and Norman Ouzts ran the ad for their music store. Thanks for the help.

CHAPTER 6

1966—Double Shot Goes National

BY NOW THE band consisted of John McElrath (the founder and "Mr. Medallion") on keyboard and vocals, Joe Morris (co-founder) on drums and vocals, Jimbo Doares on guitar and vocals, Steve Caldwell on saxophone and vocals, Brent Fortson on saxophone and vocals, Jimmy Perkins on saxophone and vocals, Charlie Webber on trumpet and vocals, and yours truly, Carroll Bledsoe, on trumpet and vocals.

We all switched around on vocals and different instruments, which gave us a lot of variety. We danced as we played and did shows and comedy routines. The horn section was then, and still is today, unique and solid. The two summers in Panama City made us a very close-knit group.

Charlie was a natural comedian. We featured him on the Coasters hit record "Along Came Jones." He played "Salty Sam," and I played "Sweet Sue." The crowd always loved it!

We signed a management and recording contract with Bill Lowery Talent out of Atlanta. Bob Richardson was head of the recording part, and Rick Carty handled the booking and management. They also handled the Tams, Billy Joe Royal, Joe South, Sandy Posey, Dennis Yost and the Classics Four, the Atlanta Rhythm Section, and others.

Our first recording was a song written by Harry Karras, who worked at Lowery. "I Want to Be Your Guy" was released on Dot Records, but it didn't do too much. We recorded several other songs written by Ray Whitley, Freddie Weller, and other writers with Lowery Talent. Freddie went on to play with Paul Revere and the Raiders and for a short time even tried country music. Ray had several big hits with the Tams. Rick Carty wrote the song "Young Love" for Tab Hunter, which was a huge hit. Many artists included the song on their albums, and Rick just kept bringing in the royalty checks, but the songs they wrote for us were just not our style of music.

Double Shot as it appeared on Smash record label.

The original copy of Double Shot on the 4 Sale label. I found this copy at a Hospice Resale Store in Landrum, S. C. in 2014. WOW!

We finally convinced them to let us record "Double Shot." They said that it was not commercial enough. We recorded it a second time using horns to replace John's organ riff. Once again, they said no.

We were getting frustrated. We knew that everywhere we played we had to play the song three or four times a night. We decided to do it our way. We went to Arthur Smith Studios in Charlotte, North Carolina, and recorded our version of "Double Shot." For those of you too young to remember, Arthur Smith and the Cracker Jacks had a popular TV show on channel 3, WBTV, in Charlotte. Their show was kind of like a country and western version of the *Lawrence Welk Show*.

We recorded the music track, then the vocals track. Last we added the party sounds. We even used some of the people working in the studio to stand around a microphone to help with the party atmosphere. It is amazing what can be done with a sixteen-track recording system.

We recorded an instrumental for the B side called "Here It Comes Again," written by John and Joe.

We had five hundred copies printed and shipped by bus to Greenwood. It was on our own label, called 4-Sale. We immediately sent copies to Dave Roddy in Birmingham.

We all stopped by radio stations as we traveled around. Joe hit the road with a box of records. Joe's wife was from Marion, South Carolina. He went to the local radio station to drop off a copy to Billy and Don Smith, two local deejays. They later became hit deejays in Myrtle Beach. He stopped in Columbia to give some copies to Woody Windom, a popular deejay in the city. Woody told Joe that he better get a lot more copies printed. When he played it on the air, the telephone lines blew up. Joe went on to Atlanta and all the surrounding towns. He was a real promoter. That summer, we outsold the Beatles, Elvis, the Rolling Stones, and everyone else in the Birmingham market.

The only negative was when he visited WQXI in Atlanta. The deejay there was Patrick Hughes, the number one deejay in Atlanta. Patrick told Joe that he received over a hundred records a week and to come back when we had a hit. He walked off without even listening to it. He had to eat his words later. I have a copy of the WQXI's top 40 list, and "Double Shot" was number one in the summer of 1966.

We soon got a call from Bob Richardson at Lowery Talent. He apologized for their error in judgment and said that they would reimburse us for all of our expenses. They also told us that they had sold the record to Mercury Records. It was being released on the Smash label, a division of Mercury.

You don't make a lot of money off of record royalties. Most of the big money comes from what you can now charge for making appearances, but royalties do help. Years after "Double Shot" left the charts, we received a call from a lawyer who had helped other artists collect past due and unpaid royalties. It wasn't long until we received a check in the mail. You are entitled not only to royalties from record sales but also from air time on the radio. A lot of artists were owed a lot of money.

At this time, Smash was primarily a soul music and rhythm and blues music label. We were invited to a Smash celebration party at a big hotel in downtown Atlanta. We got to meet Lou Rawls, Otis Redding, Joe Tex, and several others, including our friend Rufus Thomas. More on Rufus later.

We had some "Double Shot" glasses printed up and gave them out to deejays as we traveled. We would stop and visit with them and promote our record. In those days, radio stations were live, not automated as they are today. Thanks a lot, computers.

Also, as we traveled at night, we would find a pay phone (do you remember those?) and call radio stations. WOWO in Fort Wayne, Indiana, and WLS in Chicago were two such stations. They were both AM stations, and at night you could pick them up from most anywhere. We later played a show for WOWO radio, but we will talk more about that later.

We also went back to the studio in Atlanta to record our album before we hit our tour circuit. We had to cram a lot into the three summer months. If I quit teaching or the others dropped out of school, we would all be drafted.

We still had to make one more trip back to the studio. We had to dub in some new lyrics to the song before WABC in New York would play the record. We had to change the line "worst hangover that I ever had" to become "worst morning after that I ever had." "She loved me so long and she loved me so hard" became "she kissed me so long and she kissed me so hard." Compare that to the lyrics you hear on the radio today. Give me a break! Which version you got depends on when you bought your single or your album. My daughter Kelly recently found two of the albums where she lives in Sacramento, California, and she got one of each.[2]

"She Drives Me Out of My Mind was the follow-up to "Double Shot," and it also made all of the charts. We followed this up with "Hey, Hey Baby." Then came "Night Owl," "I Don't Want to Loose You, Baby," "Bye Bye Silly Girl," "Rolling, Roving River," and "I'm Gonna Hate Myself in the Morning." More about this song later.

A girl from Greenwood moved to Japan with her family. She later contacted us to say that "Double Shot" was number one over there. It was also a hit in several countries in Europe and Scandanavia. *Wow! Was this really happening to us?*

Double Shot debuts on the national charts.

---

[2] If you have one of the original 4-Sale label copies, they have sold for as much as a thousand dollars. Remember, there were only five hundred printed.

CHAPTER 7

Double Shot Tour Begins

BILL LOWERY TALENT finally realized that they had something big on their hands, bigger than they would be able to handle on their own. They could handle the southeast, but they would need help out west, up north, and in the Midwest.

They brought in Lenny Stogel & Associates out of New York City. Lenny had experience and connections all over the country. They were in charge of the tour. We hit thirty-four states in just three months. This took a lot of planning.

"Double Shot" was unusual. The record made the charts of both *Billboard* and *Cashbox* magazines, but it never made number one. It made it as high as number six and sold over a million copies. Why no number one?

We started our tour in the South and then went west. Next we hit the East Coast and finally the Midwest. We were number one in all areas, but not at the same time. Smash released the record in different areas at different times as we traveled around the country. The good news is that we stayed on the charts for twenty-three consecutive weeks. That is amazing even today.

We began our tour at the Pier in Daytona Beach, Florida, where we had played before. We were there for several days. Our agents booked a lead-off band that used equipment similar to what we used. This allowed us to pack up our gear and send our roadies across country to meet us later.

On one trip to the Pier, we played with Rufus Thomas ("The Dog" and "Walking the Dog") and became good friends. We did a show with his daughter Carla Thomas in Memphis, Tennessee, for a St. Jude's benefit. Carla was traveling alone, and Rufus asked us to look out for her. We took her back and forth to her hotel and to the airport the following day. We were now officially classified as chaperones.

We met our roadies in Tuscon, Arizona. When we landed at 5:30 p.m., the temperature was 103 degrees. Thank goodness we did not bring South Carolina's humidity with us.

We had the next day off, so we became tourists. We visited Old Tuscon, a popular film location for many western movies in those days. We visited the Desert Museum and saw giant cactus trees, prairie dogs, and other animals.

That night we decided to go to the dog races. This was a favorite pastime when we were in Daytona Beach. The track was located in the desert several miles outside of Tuscon. As guys will do, we stopped on the side of the road to relieve ourselves. *Relieve* means "pee." Soon a nice Arizona highway patrolman pulled up. He stopped not to cite us but to warn us. He explained that the desert gets very hot in the daytime but cools off rapidly at night. The rattlesnakes come out of the desert to warm themselves on the warm asphalt highway. We thanked him and did not have any more pee stops. By the way, some of us actually won a little money at the dog races.

The next night, we did our show to a great crowd. What a way to start our westward tour! The next morning, we set out driving to California, with a short stop in Mexicali, Mexico. We were not impressed, but at least we could say we had been to Mexico.

SANTA BARBARA • VENTURA • OXNARD

TOP 15 AND 20 SURVEY
week ending
JUNE 17, 1966

#	Title	Artist	Last
1	DOUBLE SHOT	SWINGING MEDALLIONS	8
2	HOLD ON I'M COMING	SAM & DAVE	4
3	DON'T BRING ME DOWN	ANIMALS	1
4	LITTLE GIRL	SYNDICATE OF SOUND	2
5	STRANGERS IN THE NIGHT	FRANK SINATRA	6
6	OH HOW HAPPY	SHADES OF BLUE	7
7	PAINT IT BLACK	ROLLING STONES	5
8	PAPERBACK WRITER	BEATLES	10
9	HANKY PANKY	TOMMY JAMES & SHONDELLS	14
10	BAREFOOTIN'	ROBERT PARKER	13
11	AIN'T TOO PROUD TOO BEG	TEMPTATIONS	17
12	SEARCHIN' FOR MY LOVE	BOBBY MOORE	19
13	SOLITARY MAN	NEIL DIAMOND	20
14	SWEET TALKIN' GUY	CHIFFONS	16
15	THE MORE I SEE YOU	CHRIS MONTEZ	9
16	ALONG COMES MARY	THE ASSOCIATION	3
17	DIRTY WATER	STANDELLS	30
18	SWEET DREAMS	TOMMY McLAIN	33
19	ELVIRA	DALLAS FRAZIER	26
20	WILD THING	THE TROGGS	NEW
21	IT'S A MAN'S WORLD	JAMES BROWN	12
22	FUNNY HOW LOVE CAN BE	DANNY HUTTON	18
23	LET'S GO GET STONED	RAY CHARLES	31
24	RED RUBBER BALL	CYRKLE	11
25	WHEN A MAN LOVES A WOMAN-	PERCY SLEDGE	15
26	POPSICLE	JAN & DEAN	27
27	DID YOU EVER HAVE TO	LOVIN' SPOONFUL	21
28	HE	RIGHTEOUS BROTHERS	NEW
29	YOU BETTER RUN	YOUNG RASCALS	NEW
30	CLOUDY SUMMER AFTERNOON	BARRY McGUIRE	22
31	OPUS 17	FOUR SEASONS	24
32	EVERYBODY NEEDS SOMEBODY TO LOVE	KNIGHTS OF DAY	NEW
33	LAND OF MILK & HONEY	THE VOGUES	NEW
34	YOU DON'T HAVE TO SAY YOU LOVE ME	DUSTY SPRINGFIELD	NEW
35	MUDDY WATER	JOHNNY RIVERS	NEW

When we arrived in Los Angeles, Double Shot was #1 on all of the area radio charts. This chart for KACY was one example.

CHAPTER 8

California, Here We Come

THE NEXT STOP was Los Angeles, California, where we were based for a week. We started out by doing a couple of local shows. One show was noteworthy because at intermission, the promoter ducked out with all of the money. Another lesson learned by eight young guys from South Carolina about the real world of the music business: *Get paid up front!*

The rest of the California experience was beyond our wildest dreams. Driving by the Hollywood sign on the mountain, the famous round Capitol Records building, Rodeo Drive, Beverly Hills … We were in California!

One day we split into two groups of four each and visited two radio stations. We were number one on all the charts all over the city. The deejay interviewed us live on the air, and then the group I was with took calls from listeners. This went on for more than an hour. Most of the calls were from young girls. Wow! We were now celebrities in Tinsel Town.

One day we taped Casey Kasem's TV show. Yes, *that* Casey Kasem of *American Top 40* fame. The show format was similar to *American Bandstand*, with lots of teenage dancers.

We took a day off to visit Disneyland. Somehow the word got out that we were there visiting the park. It could have been the paisley pants. Nevertheless, we were treated like royalty all day. We even saw a doctor and his family from Greenwood on the chairlift. They were there on vacation. As Walt Disney would say, "It's a small, small world." The Matterhorn and Space Mountain were our favorite rides.

After leaving the park, Joe, Carlie, and Jimbo rode together. On the way back to the motel from Disneyland, they got lost! They wound up at Pismo Beach with no idea how to get back the motel. They finally got back at 3:00 a.m. the next morning. A GPS system would have been nice to have back in those days.

The following two days were unbelievable! Thank you, Lenny Stogel. First, we were flown to Monterey, California, and then motored over to Big Sur. There we taped Dick Clark's show *Where the Action Is*.

We flew up with Percy Sledge, who was going to be on the same show. Brent and Joe spent a large portion of the flight talking with Percy. It seems this was Percy's first time on an airplane, and he was a little bit nervous. We also met Steve Alamo, a regular on the show, and the Action Dancers.

As we were getting ready to perform for the taping, we heard a group of girls talking. One of them said, "They don't even have long hair." Remember, this was at the peak of the British invasion of the music world. After the taping, these same girls loved it. They especially liked our signature dance routine in the middle of "Double Shot." The band still does the same routine today.

We had to join several unions to be able to appear on national TV. We were already members of the American Federation of Musicians. They had a representative waiting for us at every performance to collect their local dues. Don't get me started on unions. More on this subject later.

The union would allow only six of us to appear on TV. John and Joe agreed to sit out since they were not a part of the dance routine. We were all upset about this. I still don't understand to this very day their reasoning.

THE SWINGIN MEDALLIONS 1966

Our world famous, or should I say infamous, green and gold paisley pants. They got us noticed at Disney Land and made a big impression on Milton Berle.

I have saved the biggest thrill for last. We played Tina Sinatra's sixteenth birthday party at the Hillcrest Country Club in Beverly Hills. Tina is Nancy Sinatra's younger sister. There were four hundred or more guests, and it was like a who's who list of Hollywood.

As we were setting up, several members of the Rat Pack were finishing up a round of golf. One of our amplifiers went out. The agent who had booked us was Milton Berle's nephew. He said that he could help us out. About an hour later, a van pulled up with two huge Standel amps. The men said that Mr. Sinatra had sent them over. When we finished, we asked what we needed to do with the amps. We were told to keep them—they were ours.

That night, we were introduced by the one and only Milton Berle. We were wearing yellow Gant shirts and our green and gold paisley pants. He commented that it was the first time he had ever introduced a group who were wearing their pajamas.

We did our forty-five-minute set and retired to the bar. I think we all needed a drink. Steve and Brent had to have Cokes because they were underage. Soon, Frank Sinatra came in to talk to us. He asked if we were being taken good care of. They had a local band playing after us. Frank said that everyone loved our show. He asked if we could possibly play some more. We did two more sets.

Frank Sinatra, Nancy Sinatra, Frank Sinatra Jr., Jack Benny, Barbara Stanwick, Milton Berle, and of course the Rat Pack—Peter Lawford, Joey Bishop, and Sammie Davis Jr. were there. The only one missing was Dean Martin. I believe he was performing in Las Vegas.

It was the only time that I can remember being scared before a performance. I think that we all were. What could we do to impress all of these icons? We had watched them on TV and in movies all of our lives, and now we were entertaining them. We must have done something right because they loved it.

Frank had his own record label, Reprise Records. He called our agents and wanted to sign us, but we had just signed with Smash, so that was the end of that.

Photoplay magazine did an article on the party in their next issue. We were a prominent part of the article.

I have always felt that your hometown crowd is the hardest crowd to impress and play for. You grow up with these people. They know you. I must admit that our hometown crowd is the best and most supportive. They are happy and proud of whatever success we have achieved.

But when you are on the road with a hit record and a hit album, you are just as big a celebrity as anyone, even in Los Angeles. We never did get used to the screaming teenage girls, all the autographs, all the photographs, and all the interviews, but we all loved every minute of it. We just could not believe that all of this was happening.

CHAPTER 9

Oregon and Washington

CALIFORNIA WAS BEHIND us, and we were headed for the great Northwest. The first stop was Portland, Oregon. We did a one-night show for a deejay. He showed us around town before and after the show.

Seattle, Washington, was our next stop. We were based out of there for a week. We would go out to a different location in the surrounding area each day. One stop that we made was at Old Orchard Beach, Washington. I think the word *beach* is a little bit of a stretch. To us, it was mostly mud with a little sand. This was probably not being fair because we were comparing it to Panama City beach and Myrtle Beach back home. Not many beaches can stack up against these two.

The last part of the week we played a club at a hotel in Seattle. Once again we had a local front band with equipment similar to ours. Our roadies hit the road for the trip all the way back across the country. The last night at the club, Joe ran out of drumsticks. He gave the drummer of the local band some money to purchase some new ones. Guess what? The drummer forgot. Joe took two wooden coat hangers and removed the wooden rods at the bottom of each hanger. These rods became his drumsticks for the night. Joe said, "You got to do what you've got to do."

We did a little sightseeing in the area. We took an afternoon trip to Canada one day. We also had lunch on top of the Space Needle in its revolving restaurant. We were there to celebrate Brent Fortson's eighteenth birthday. The Space Needle was built as the showpiece of the Seattle World's Fair. By the way, whatever happened to world's fairs? Why did they disappear?

We were a long way from home, and I think a lot of us were beginning to miss good old South Carolina. After our week in Seattle, we would be heading back in that direction.

This article is from the Columbia, S. C. State newspaper. It is dated May 1, 1966. We have made the big times in our state capital city!

CHAPTER 10

Atlanta, Georgia, Y'all

WE MET OUR road crew and, more importantly, our families and friends in Atlanta, Georgia, on July 4, 1966.

We were set to do a show in Atlanta Fulton County Stadium, home of the Braves and the Falcons. The show consisted of us, James Brown, and an English group—the Who? The Guess Who? Or Who Knows Who? I can't remember. There were over 28,000 fans in attendance. It was the largest crowd we had ever played for.

Since we recorded and booked out of Atlanta, it was almost like coming home. All of the crowd from Lowery Talent came out to visit with us. Rick Carty, Ray Whitley, Bob Richardson, and others all showed up. We dressed in the Braves home dressing room.

We went on first. James Brown and members of his band sat in the home dugout while we performed. They watched our entire show. One of our roadies heard James Brown tell his band to watch our horn section. He told them to take notes on how we moved and danced. He was impressed and wanted them to work on that. James was also the one, we found out later, that recommended to Bob Richardson that Smash be our record label.

James was sort of responsible for Smash Records being born. He had a dispute with King Records and decided to leave the King label. Shelby Singleton, an executive at Mercury Records, founded Smash Records as a subsidiary to Mercury in 1969. It was run by him and Charlie Fach. Fach took over in 1966, but the company closed for good in 1996.

All of James Brown's instrumentals from 1964 to 1967 were on Smash as were three of his vocal releases. Among the artists to appear on Smash were James Brown, Jay and the Techniques, Jerry

Lee Lewis, Frankie Valli, Roger Miller, and of course the Swingin' Medallions.

As you can see, Smash Records had a large variety of artists, from country to pop to rock 'n' roll. It was an honor to be included with such high-profile artists.[3]

---

[3] Smash Records information from Wikipedia.

CHAPTER 11

East Coast Tour Begins

AFTER A COUPLE of days off at home with our families, we headed to Charlotte, North Carolina, where we did a show for the Big Ways radio station. Big Ways was one of several radio stations across the country who reported their play list each week to BMI. These reports were combined and compared to get an average play list all across the country. This list was used to get chart ratings for Billboard and Cashbox magazines and, more importantly to us, the royalties due to us. We made number one in Charlotte.

Even if a station did not play a particular song on the air, they would be held responsible for the average play count across the country. Even if they played it more than the average, they were still charged only with the average play count. At least this was how it was explained to us.

Next up was Richmond, Virginia, another magical event for us. We were booked at the Coliseum for a matinee show and an evening show. We were on the bill along with Mitch Ryder and the Detroit Wheels and the Dave Clark Five, who were the headliners.

We opened the show that afternoon and were followed by Mitch Ryder. We put on our usual forty-five-minute set, and the crowd ate it up. That night, Mitch Ryder went to the promoter and demanded to go on first. He would not follow us again.

During the break between shows, some of us went to the concession stand to get a bite to eat. A group of girls in the hall spotted us. We had to run with our food back to the dressing room, losing several hairs out of our heads that the girls grabbed for souvenirs. Who in the world started that fad? *Ouch!* The next morning, the Richmond newspaper had an article about the show. The article took up over half of a full page. The article began "Mitch Ryder rocked them, Dave Clark wowed them, but the group that stole the show was the Swingin' Medallions." The rest of the article was all about us. They loved the horns, the dancing, the variety, and the showmanship. Eat your heart out, Mitch Ryder!

CHAPTER 12

We Love You, Too, Pittsburgh

ON TO THE steel city of Pittsburgh, Pennsylvania we went for two days of engagements. The first night, we made promotional appearances at a chain of Red Rooster nightclubs. These clubs are spread out over the area, and we covered three of them that night. "Double Shot" was number one in Pittsburgh at this time.

The next day we had an afternoon and an evening show scheduled at Kennywood Amusement Park, one of the earliest large amusement parks, very similar to Six Flags parks. That morning the park's manager and young daughter took us on a tour of the park.

We found out that the agent who booked us had only heard our record. He thought that we were a singing group. As a result, he hired some union musicians to back us up. We were scheduled for a forty-five-minute show that afternoon and another forty-five-minute show that evening. We had to give the union guys fifteen minutes at each show. There's that union thing again.

The shows were held in an outdoor amphitheater. That afternoon there was a good crowd, but that night there were thousands. Our dressing rooms were located underneath the stage. After the show, we were changing when a policeman came in. He asked if we would mind signing a few autographs so that the crowd would disperse and leave. We said yes, of course. We signed autographs for over an hour and still had to have a police escort to get to our cars.

By the way, the park manager's daughter sent me and my family a Christmas card that year. She sent us a card every year until she was well into her twenties. She kept us informed with what was going on in her life. You just never know what affect you will have on someone's life. I will always have a special place in my heart for Pittsburgh.

CHAPTER 13

New York, New York

NEXT UP WAS New York City. We spent three days there doing publicity work with Lenny Stogel and his agency. We also began planning another tour with some of his other groups.

We were too busy for much sightseeing. I remember Broadway, Radio City Music Hall, and what seemed like at least a million yellow taxicabs. In New York, you take the subway or you catch a cab. Those are your only two choices. No one drives in New York City. And there is not a single thrill ride at any amusement park in the country that compares to a taxi ride in New York City.

One time Brent was running late for a meeting, so he hailed a cab. When he got into the cab, it already had one passenger—Neil Diamond. They chatted during the ride, and Brent told Neil he was from South Carolina. It could be just a coincidence, but not long after that, Neil recorded "Sweet Caroline."

One night some of us took in a movie. The theatre was nice but nothing special. But you could smell marijuana in the air. The movie was *2001: A Space Odyssey*. After the show, several people outside were asking anyone they could find to explain the movie to them. They were totally confused.

After New York came New England: New Hampshire, Connecticut, Maine, and Rhode Island. I remember one thing in particular about Maine. We played at the beach. Back home at the beach, you could buy a cup of french fries. Up here you could buy a cup of fried clams. They were delicious.

We attended our first horse race in Rhode Island. Most of us still preferred the dog races. You simply bet on a lightweight dog if the track is dry and a heavier dog if the track is wet—and for one other reason: It's hard to fix a dog race.

The countryside in New England was beautiful. Most of the people we met there were nicer and more laid back than the ones in New York City. But they still teased us about our accent.

CHAPTER 14

Buses, Planes, and Automobiles

*B*USES: LENNY SET up a bus tour with us and some of his other groups. We went to Columbia and Greenville, South Carolina, Birmingham, and Panama City. As you probably noticed, all of these cities were our old stomping grounds. We were the headliners for a change.

On the show with us were Sam the Sham and the Pharoahs, Napoleon the Fourteenth, and a young English group. Sam the Sham loved to play poker. That's all he did on the bus. I have no clue as to who won, but Brent claims he took Sam to the cleaners.

Another bus story has to be included. On one trip to Birmingham, we saw an old Trailways bus for sale. The bus's owner was a mechanic and a preacher. Beware of that combination. We bought the bus, had it painted, and had metal bunk beds installed. The bus did great for a while, but it finally died in Waycross, Georgia. The former owner had put sawdust in the rear end and transmission to disguise its mechanical flaws. We donated the bus to a car repair shop there in Waycross.

While the bus was still active, we played at Virginia Military Institute for their senior farewell party. We didn't really think of VMI as a party school, but they changed our minds. As we walked around the campus, we could hear our album blasting from multiple dorm room windows.

The party was held in a field far off from campus. There was a three-sided building for the band to set up, including several other bands. It all started at 11:00 a.m. and continued into the wee hours of the next morning. The guys had been in a strict military school for four years, and they were ready to party. Several tried to use our bus for a rendezvous with their dates, but Charlie guarded the door to the bus diligently.

Planes: We had several adventures with planes. On several occasions we had bookings during the year when school was in session. Our hero and rescue pilot was Mike Langford from Greenwood. His father owned Langford flying service at the Greenwood County Airport. Once Mike flew me to Varnville, South Carolina, for a show at the Varnville swimming pool. We left after school and flew to Allendale-Fairfax County Airport. Sid Vaughn owned the pool, which was always packed.

Another time Mike flew Brent and me to Memphis, Tennessee, for a show. There may have been other trips, but I remember these two.

We cut up with the flight attendants on the flight to Hawaii. Charlie and Jimbo kept them entertained the entire flight.

But by far the most interesting flight came after a one-night show in Hopkinsville, Kentucky. The next day we were scheduled to play a show for WOWO radio in Fort Wayne, Indiana. We thought that the show was at night. Our agent called and said that the show was at 2:00 p.m., not 8:00 p.m. They chartered two twin engine planes to get us there.

We took off in a light fog, but the fog got much worse. At first we could see our other plane out of the window, but then we lost sight of it in the fog. Then the plane I was on lost all of its radios. We had to land in Lexington, Kentucky, for repairs.

Our roadies had driven all night. Despite this, we all made it in time for the show. Whew!

Automobiles: Now for the automobiles part. We were booked in Clear Lake, Iowa. We played the same arena where Buddy Holly, Richie Valins, and the Big Bopper played their last show before the plane crash took all of their lives.

We had only two days to make our next show—in Galveston, Texas. Do you have any idea how far that is by car? The booking agents had struck again. But we made it. We even took time to visit the world famous Iowa State Fair on the way. Lawrence Welk was the headliner. We did not have time to stay for his show. I guess we'll have to catch him on television.

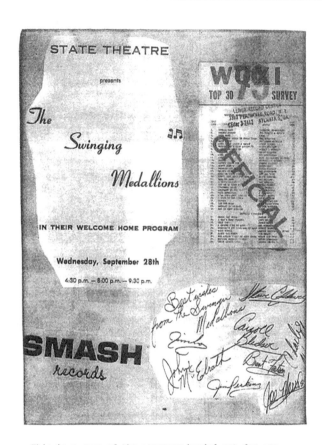

This is a copy of the programs handed out for our welcome home party and performance. A small side note about WQXI Top 30 Survey. Pat Hughes, the #1 dee jay in Atlanta who had snubbed Joe Morris had to eat crow when Double Shot became #1 at his station.

CHAPTER 15

Welcome Home

AT THE END of the summer of 1966, we returned home and were greeted with a nice surprise. The State Theater, a movie theater in downtown Greenwood, was chosen as the location. The mayor of Greenwood, John Nave, had declared it Swingin' Medallions Day in Greenwood. It was like a Hollywood movie premier, complete with a spotlight and a red carpet. We were driven up in limousines. Actually, they were family cars from Blyth Funeral Home, where my father happened to work for over forty years. He had also worked a short time at Cox Funeral Home in Belton, South Carolina. My parents lived in a garage apartment behind the funeral home. So yes, I was born in a funeral home! That helps explain why sometimes I do things backward.

Anyway, the mayor presented each of us with the key to the city and a copy of the proclamation. Fifty years later, in September of 2016, Mayor Weldon Adams presented us with a proclamation celebrating fifty years of "Double Shot" and the Swingin' Medallions at a downtown live event. Joe Morris, Bent Fortson, John McElrath, and I were all there. Of course, Jimmy Perkins was there since he has rejoined the group, and Larry Roark is back playing keyboard.

On June 28, 2013, the town of Ninety Six also presented us with the key to the city and a proclamation. John and Joe were both born and raised in Ninety Six. Mayor Arvest Turner made the presentation to each of us, including several former members from over the years. Many old friends and former classmates were there as well.

In late 1966, after our tour ended, that Steve Caldwell and Brent Fortson left the group. They started a band called the Pieces of Eight. Steve's father, Earl Caldwell, was behind all of this.

The Pieces of Eight
Earl Caldwell convinced Brent Fortson and Steve Caldwell to start a new group but they tried to confiscate the name "Swingin' Medallions" to go along with their name The Pieces of Eight.

They released a record called "Lonely Drifter." On the label was written "Pieces of Eight—The Original Swingin' Medallions." He had convinced Steve and Brent that this would double the impact of both groups. In reality, he felt that since he had booked us two summers in Panama City, he owned the name and all of the rights. This resulted in a federal lawsuit over who owned the name. We won the case in federal court in Columbia, South Carolina.

This brings up the story of our love for unions again. We sent the AFM union a letter requesting their help with the case. After all those years of paying dues, they not only didn't provide any help, we didn't even get a reply from them. Thanks a lot, guys. We can take your dues and shove it!

CHAPTER 16

Aloha!

HOW WOULD YOU like a vacation in Hawaii? How about two months in Hawaii and still have money to send home? This is what we did in the summer of 1967. We were booked at the Dunes Supper Club in Honolulu, Hawaii, for a month. Then we were held over for a second month.

A Mr. and Mrs. Davies owned a wooden two-story apartment complex right on Waikiki Beach. They were located between the Hawaiian Hilton and the Ilikai hotels. Each apartment had a kitchen, living area, and a room for two to sleep. We stayed two people per apartment, and it cost only seventy-five dollars per week for each of us. Try to find a deal like that in Myrtle Beach, even in 1967. Due to the location, we had access to all of the amenities and restaurants of both hotels. The Hilton even had a private lagoon.

The owner of the Dunes had a large complex consisting of a country music club, a Las Vegas style burlesque club, and the supper club. Something for everyone was his motto. The supper club was upscale and modeled after what you might find in Las Vegas. In fact, a lot of the dancers in the burlesque club rotated between Las Vegas and Honolulu. Everything was first class. They were located near the airport in a good section of town.

The owner was also helpful in giving us ideas as to how to put together a Las Vegas style show. He had a good background in this area due to all of his Las Vegas connections.

The bouncers at our club were all great big Samoans called *Hawlies*. We called them our gentle giants. They normally looked down on tourists, but they took a liking to us, and this turned out to be great as time went by. We had Mondays off, and so did they. They took us places the average tourist never gets to see.

One Monday they took us inland to a very, very tall waterfall on the side of a mountain. They (not us) would climb up to the top of the falls, then would pick leaves from a native plant and pack them into their mouths. They did this to prevent their sinus cavities from bursting when they dove off of these high cliffs. It was amazing to witness these feats.

Another time they took us to a bay in which there was a large coral reef. We all went snorkeling and saw the many colors of fish! It was like swimming in an aquarium. Blue, yellow, orange, red, white, multicolored, you name it—they were there. Thank goodness we never saw a shark or an electric eel.

As an interesting side note, we learned from them that on the island of Oahu there are no snakes. This is an island formed from a volcano. Snakes had no way to get there.

On another trip we went to the North Shore. This is where most of the competitive surfing you see on TV takes place. We had never seen waves that big before.

The beach at Waikiki is beautiful. We learned from our Samoan friends that we all needed to purchase a pair of flip-flops. The sand on the beach is coarse, not soft and powdery like back home. The sand will chew up the bottoms of your feet.

Hawaii's main crop is pineapple. Most all other food is imported. Therefore, food in grocery stores and restaurants can be one of a visitor's biggest expenses. Our pals steered us to several diners where most of the locals eat. This helped us out a lot. Another big expense is an automobile. You had to either rent or borrow a car to get around.

One of John and my favorite restaurants was the Tahitian Lanai, an outdoor restaurant at the Hawaiin Hilton. One of our favorite dishes was fried bananas. They would take a whole banana, peel it, dip it in a batter, and deep fry it like a corn dog. Unbelievable!

And yes, one Monday night we went to see the Don Ho Show, complete with his song "Tiny Bubbles." We also got to see hula dancers at a luau and caught a great concert at the Ilikia by the 5th Dimension.

After a week or so, we brought the wives over for a visit. Just like us, they had never been to Hawaii. We showed them around. It was really good to see them.

Having the wives over did create some homesickness in the guys. Charlie and Jimbo decided that it was time to head home. We brought in Gerald Polk on keyboard and trumpet. Gerald had been a school band director in Walterboro, South Carolina. He had also played in a popular group called the Melody Makers. These guys became friends of ours. Their drummer, Ronnie Nobles, later played drums with us.

To replace Jimbo on guitar, we brought in David Easler from back home. David was a pleasant and talented eighteen-year-old. This had to be the biggest thrill of his young life. Can you imagine being eighteen, playing with a well-known band, and your first gig is playing for a month in Hawaii?

Tragically, shortly after we returned home, David was killed in a car wreck while heading to a party at Lake Greenwood. His parents thanked us for giving him this opportunity. They said that he had never been happier. This loss was so, so, sad for all of us.

CHAPTER 17

A Battle of Accents

OUR BOOKING AGENTS struck again: They booked us to play in Boston over the Christmas holidays. This was both good and bad.

The first week we played in a beautiful club out in Manchester. It attracted a predominately college crowd. Since it was the Christmas holidays, two families got together and invited us to Christmas dinner, showing real southern hospitality all the way up north in Boston.

The day we arrived was the same day of their first snowfall of the year. We did not see the ground again until we left town two weeks later. We stayed at a snow-covered beach. What's up with that? We took the MTA (subway) to work every day.

One thing was evident from day one: our southern accents. We stood out everywhere we went. We laughed just as hard at their Boston brogue. At times, we almost needed translators.

As good as the first week was, the second week was equally bad. We were booked into the Downtown Lounge, a club in the middle of the Combat Zone, an infamous area of Boston. We could not wait to get out of there every night. It was a completely different and rougher crowd than anywhere we had ever played before. They liked us, but they were nothing like the crowds we were used to playing for. We left the club each night as a group for safety reasons. For the very first time, this began to feel like work.

There was one bright side, however. Bob Lee's Chinese restaurant was located nearby. It was the best Chinese restaurant I had ever been to. They had just finished a million-dollar renovation to the interior. They even put in a waterfall on one wall. A million dollars in 1967 was a lot of money. Our favorite dish was called a *pu pu platter*. This dish had a sampling of many different items.

We had time to do a little sightseeing. Of course, this included Fenway Park, home of the Boston Red Sox.

The Swingin' Medallions as seen in the movie Mondo Daytona. It is hard to be seen in a movie if you cannot find the movie to see.

CHAPTER 18

Mondo Daytona

During the 1960s, a movie was released called *Mondo Caine*, a documentary about something. I have no idea what that something was, but the theme song from the movie became a big hit. Bill Lowery Talent decided to make a movie featuring some of the groups they represented.

Johnny Cox of Enoree, South Carolina, and Hack Bartley of Greenwood had joined the band. Johnny played saxophone, keyboard, flute, or just about anything. He was a fantastic musician. Hack played saxophone and did vocals. Hack was a great showman and dancer. Years later, Hack formed his own band, Hack Bartley and Shuffle. They recorded several beach music hits. Hack's son Jake was in his band, and later on, Jake joined the Swingin' Medallions.

But let's get back to *Mondo Daytona*. The movie was a documentary about spring break in Daytona Beach. The crew followed the college crowd, filming huge parties that were held on the world famous beach. They also visited various nightclubs and of course the Pier, our old stomping ground. We spent several days in town and got to renew our fascination with the dog races. It was sprinkled with music videos by the Tams, Billy Joe Royals, the Swingin' Medallions, and a few others. The movie was so popular that it never even played in our home town. We had to drive to Greenville, South Carolina, to see it at a drive-in movie. So much for a career in Hollywood!

One former Medallion did make it in Hollywood—Grainger Hines, or Brother Hines as I knew him. Grainer appeared in several movies and numerous TV shows. He was on *Matlock* and several other shows as a guest star. He was also a regular on the prime time soap opera *Dynasty*. Brother started out as a member of our road crew. He taught himself to play the baritone sax. He was a handsome dude and all the girls loved him. He was married for a while to Michelle Phillips of Mamas and Papas fame.

Speaking of the dog races, we picked up a few helpful hints on how to pick a winning dog. Each race has eight dogs competing. They usually have eleven races each night and matinee races two times a week. We mentioned earlier how to pick a dog due by its weight and the track conditions. Before each race they would parade the dogs in front of the grandstand. If a dog stopped to relieve itself (doing number two), you should bet on that dog. Bettors can be a superstitious group.

CHAPTER 19

Don't Worry, Jesse, We Will Get You Out

THIS PARTICULAR SITUATION is comical now, but it was not very funny at the time. We had been on the road touring several colleges in Virginia. Playing colleges usually meant getting paid by check. John and I usually carried money with us, but some of the guys believed that they would be able to get by on the money we would get paid on the road. This time we came up short.

John and I both had spent most of our cash on gas, meals, motels, and so forth. In those days, the speed limits on most interstates and some regular roads ranged from 65 to 75 mph. Not in Virginia. The speed limit there, even on an interstate highway, was 55 mph. We had played in Blacksburg, Virginia, and were headed for our last stop on this trip in Roanoke, Virginia. We had enough gas money to get home, and that was about it.

We got pulled over by a Virginia highway patrolman for doing 65 mph. I was driving. He wrote us a ticket and said that we could follow him back to Blacksburg and pay the fine of two hundred dollars. It may as well have been two *thousand* dollars. We tried to explain, but he was having none of it. We followed him back, and I was arrested. Saturday afternoon and in jail is no place you want to be.

John knew of a friend he used to work with at the YMCA in Greenwood who now lived near Blacksburg. John called him to get him to wire the money, which he said he would be glad to do. John and the others planned to cheer me up. They stood outside the jail's second-story window, where I was located, and began chanting: "Don't worry, Jesse; we will get you out of there. They can't hold you."

We soon found out that it would take several hours to wire the money. Our friend told John and the others to go on to Roanoke. He said he would bring the money and then bring me to Roanoke. This worked and we all made the show, but it was a very, very, long day.

The patrolman even came back to my cell and apologized. He said that he thought we were just pretending to now have the money.

CHAPTER 20

The Wreck

DURING ALL OF our years and miles of traveling, we were fortunate to avoid car accidents. One happened, though. We were driving from Greenwood, South Carolina, to Birmingham, Alabama, to do a show for Dave Roddy. There was no Interstate 20 from Atlanta to Birmingham as there is today, so we had to take the backroads. We went through Marietta, Georgia, and on to Dallas, Georgia.

It was raining, thank goodness, so we were driving slowly. A car pulled up to a stop sign, stopped, and then pulled right out in front of us. We hit them in the driver's door. Both the driver and the passenger were ejected into a muddy ditch. Thanks to the rain and mud, they would survive. Charlie and Jimbo were in the back seat. Charlie stuck his foot through the back of my seat and cut it pretty badly. Jimbo was not hurt. I was wearing my seat belt, but in those days it was only a lap belt. I hit the steering wheel with my head and chest hard enough to bend the steering wheel. The two men in the car we hit had a bottle of moonshine between them in the front seat before the crash.

After we got out of the car, Charlie kept telling me that we needed to go into a nearby house and wash my face. A dirty face was the least of my worries. He kept insisting, and I finally agreed. When I looked into the mirror, I saw my face was covered in blood. I had a gash in my left eyelid that required thirteen stiches to close. A half an inch lower would have ruptured my eyeball. They loaded Charlie and me into the ambulance and took us to the hospital to get fixed up. I also had badly bruised ribs, but thankfully, none were broken. Charlie wound up on crutches for a while.

We spent the night in an old hotel in downtown Atlanta. The bed was so high that I had to have help getting in due to my ribs.

The two men had both been drunk. The police told us that if we wanted to sue them, we would have to get in line and take a number. You meet the nicest people in the darnedest places, don't you? The wreck made the news all over Birmingham, Greenwood, and most of the southeast.

The next day we caught a Southern Airways DC-3 back to Greenwood, with stops in Athens, Georgia, and Anderson, South Carolina. The trip took three hours. You can drive it in two and a half hours.

When we came off the plane, we looked like we were returning from a war. Charlie was on crutches. I had a patch over my eye and was hobbling due to my ribs. We made it to the show later. The crowd was glad to see that we were OK.

CHAPTER 21

LSU

THERE WAS ONE more fraternity party that I have to single out. This one took place at LSU, in Baton Rouge, Louisiana. Have you ever seen Tiger Stadium? It's so large there were dormitory rooms under one end of the stadium.

By this time we were way too expensive for one fraternity to afford to fly us down to Baton Rouge for a one-night show, so the guys at LSU came up with a brilliant idea. They got together with a neighboring fraternity on fraternity row to book us for the weekend. The TKE fraternity guys were the masterminds behind this idea, and they worked out all the details.

Here is how it all worked: When our roadies arrived on Friday, they set up at the neighboring fraternity. We played there Friday night. After the show, the Tekes had all of their fraternity pledges carry our equipment back to their house. We were given the use of the pledges' rooms for the night. This saved them the expense of putting us up in a motel. They had the pledges stay up all night to guard our equipment.

On Saturday night, we played for the Tekes in their house. They came up with the idea of having us play from 5:00 p.m. until 8:00 p.m. instead of normal hours. Then they loaded us up and drove us to New Orleans for the last night of Mardi Gras. Needless to say, we were up all night. They hung around to show us where to go and, more importantly, where not to go. We spent most of the night listening to Danny White and his band. Then they took us to the airport to catch our 8:30 a.m. plane back to Greenwood.

The guys at LSU should be highly commended for their ingenuity and attention to detail. It could not have gone any better. We really appreciated all of the great hospitality. Don't you love it when a plan comes together? *Geaux Tigers!*

A little later on we played a week at a club in Dallas, Texas. We were there for a week. They had a house band that opened for us each night, with a guitar player named Bobbie Taylor. Bobbie was a great musician and a soulful vocalist. Bobbie later joined the Medallions. After leaving the Medallions, he went on tour with Percy Sledge for several years.

We also played a beautiful club up on a mountain in Chattanooga, Tennessee. The club was owned by Billy Hull, a former professional football player for the Green Bay Packers. He was a super-nice guy with a beautiful club. A lot of big-name acts had their pictures on the walls there, and we were honored to join the list.

CHAPTER 22

Return to Myrtle Beach

I HAD NOT been back to Myrtle Beach since my high school and college days, but that was soon to change. We began to play regularly at the Beach Club on Highway 17, north of Myrtle Beach. It was one of the few places on the grand strand that featured live bands. It was there during my younger days, too, but as I mentioned, we had no fake IDs.

Cecil Corbett was the owner. He was a great guy to work with, and we always looked forward to playing there. The crowds were always large, and the dance floor was packed.

Sometimes we were the only group performing. Sometimes we had company. One week we played with Lou Christie, who had the hit record "Lightning Is Striking Again." Another time we played with Robert Knight, who had the hit record "Everlasting Love." Robert was another super-nice guy. He was also a school teacher, so he and I had something in common. This was his first hit record and his first public appearance. We tried to help him all we could and back him up musically. We also played with Willie T, who had the hit record "Thank You, John." Other groups that appeared there included the Temptations, Jerry Butler, and Jackie Wilson.

Our favorite by far was Clifford Curry of Knoxville, Tennessee. His hits included "She Shot a Hole in My Soul" and "I'm Gonna Hate Myself in the Morning." In later years we made our own recording of "I'm Gonna Hate Myself in the Morning." Clifford returned the favor by recording his version of "Double Shot." I still have the 45 of his version. Clifford passed away recently. The current band played a tribute show in Knoxville. We will all miss you, my friend.

Swingin' Medallion reunion at the Atlanta Country Club in the mid 1980's. This was another Gregg Haynes Production.

From Left to Right: Charlie Webber, John McElrath, Jimbo Doares, Joe Morris, Brent Fortson, Steve Caldwell and Carroll Bledsoe.

CHAPTER 23

Friends Along the Way

WE MET SEVERAL great friends along our journey. Bobby Bowick was from Alabama and a graduate of Auburn University. We met Bobby while we were playing in Panama City, Florida. Bobby was a loyal fan and a good friend who followed us when he could. He was instrumental in getting us to play at Auburn. Bobby also worked on the staff of Governor George Wallace. He arranged for all of us to receive certificates certifying that each of us was an honorary colonel in the Alabama militia. He also gave each of us an Auburn football team jersey. Mine was number 23. Thanks for everything, Bobby.

Gregg Haynes of Waycross, Georgia, became a big fan and a great friend of ours. He promoted a big show with us at the City Auditorium in Waycross. The mayor proclaimed it Swingin' Medallions Day in the city. April 18, 1968, was the date of the first show. We came back and did two more shows for Gregg within six months. Four thousand tickets were sold for the three shows. That's a lot of tickets for a town the size of Waycross. The auditorium was rocking.

At one of these shows, the weather was cold and rainy. We were gathered in the dressing room before the show when Charlie Webber came in. He announced that he wanted to collect ten dollars from each of us. It turned out that Charlie had been outside and had seen a young boy and girl selling boiled peanuts. Neither one of them had on any shoes. Charlie gave the money to their father. Charlie told him that when we come back, he had better not find out that he did not buy the children some new shoes. Remember, Charlie was an ex-college fullback. I think the father got his message.

In later years, Gregg also promoted several Medallion reunion shows. One of the first and largest was held at Chastain Park in Atlanta, Georgia. This was a fun weekend, and it was fun to get the guys back together. He set it up for us to visit several nightclubs the evening before our concert to promote the event. Gregg did not miss a trick when he put on an event. The park was packed.

A little side note: After the show, my wife and I were standing on the stage visiting with fans when a well-endowed young lady came up to us. She had a bumper sticker that read I Love Beach Music and stuck it on her shirt across her bosom. She said to me "I want your autograph right here." I looked at Gail, and she said, "Go ahead, have a little fun," so I did. Can you imagine how hard it is to sign an autograph in that location?

Gregg promoted several other shows for us in the Atlanta area. One that I remember was at the Atlanta Country Club. I have the picture from that night. It was one of the last times Steve and Charlie were able to perform with us.

Gregg became a big fan of Southern beach music. He published a beautiful coffee table book entitled *The Heeey Baby Days of Beach Music*. In the book he has photos and stories of just about every group you could imagine. Some of the information in this book is based on information in Gregg's book. If you are a fan, it would be well worth it for you to purchase a copy of this book. Find it online or wherever you can. You will treasure it for years. Gregg presented each of us with an autographed copy, and I certainly treasure mine.

We continue to meet many fans today from our past. I played with the Medallions this summer (2017) in Greenville, South Carolina, at Chiefs Wings and Firewater. A man came up to me and introduced himself. He had friends in Greenville but he was from California. In 1966 he was a deejay out there and had played and loved our record. He had come all this way to relive many wonderful memories.

I went to my high school reunion in Greenwood in August 2017. A classmate of mine had been in Seattle, Washington, at the same time we were. He lived in Los Angeles at the time. He remembered driving on the freeway in LA and hearing "Double Shot" come on the radio.

He told me that the deejay commented that "Double Shot" was a party that we somehow were able to capture on a record. That is as good a compliment as one could get.

Over the years, we have held several Medallion reunions at the Civic Center in Greenwood. Each one was like going to a school reunion. We saw people we had not seen in years. Some of these shows helped raise money for local charities. One was sponsored by the Greenwood Humane Society. They even set up a special pre-dance VIP lounge. People could pay extra and mingle with the band members and their friends.

One such show was very special. US Congressman Gresham Barrett was there. He presented John McElrath with the Order of the Palmetto, the highest order our state can present to someone. We were all very proud to be a part of this event. Gresham has remained a friend and was later to become a customer of mine when I was in wholesale sales. He is a loyal and true friend. He attended my grandson's wedding in Seneca, South Carolina, in 2016.

CHAPTER 24

Jekyll Island—2006

AT THE JEKYLL Island Beach Music Festival, the entire weekend was a tribute celebrating forty years of "Double Shot of My Baby's Love." Along with the Medallions, there were performances by The Tams and Hack Bartley and Shuffle. We did a show Friday night. A Saturday afternoon concert was interrupted by a thunderstorm. It was being held outside on the beach. The Tams were able to get their performance in before they had to clear the beach. We had to cancel our performance.

We did another show and dance that evening. All through the weekend there was a crew filming a documentary about us. Andrea Powell Ambrose was in charge of the filming. They filmed all of our performances and also numerous interviews with each one of us individually. They showed part of the film before one of our reunion shows in Greenwood. Andrea had planned on airing the film on Georgia and South Carolina PBS TV Channels.

Secrets of the South is a regional magazine for this area. The magazine contained a long article about the band. Pabst Blue Ribbon beer, Coors beer, and 107.9—Coast Radio—all had full-page ads congratulating us for four years of "Double Shot." The Pabst ad said "a double toast to 'Double Shot.'" I thought that was pretty cool!

A special thanks goes out to Sonny Dixon, a "Southern secret and news anchor legend." Sonny was a big supporter of the band in the past and throughout the weekend.

Bruce Springstein promotion flyer. He mentions that amoung the influences on his music career were Elvis Presley, Gary U. S. Bonds, and the Swingin' Medallions.

CHAPTER 25

Tooting Our Own Horns

IN ADDITION TO John receiving the Order of the Palmetto, the band was fortunate enough to be recognized with several honors, awards, and accolades.

James Brown himself recommended the Smash record label to Bill Lowery Talent. He said that they would be a good fit for "Double Shot" to be distributed nationally.

A few years back, Bruce Springsteen did a show at the auditorium in Greenville. He invited some Swingin' Medallions to appear on stage with him. Bruce has always listed his greatest influences in music as: Elivs Presley, Gary U. S. Bonds, the Swingin' Medallions, and a cast of thousands. This is quite the compliment!

Bruce was joined on stage by Grainger Hines, Jimmy Perkins, Shawn McElrath, and Brent Fortson to perform "Double Shot" with him. Joe Morris was also there, but Joe has some of my bad luck. According to Brent, when they called the guys up on stage to perform, Joe was in the restroom. By the time he got there, security would not let him on stage. What a bummer! I really feel for Joe, but at least he was there—and I was not. The other guys will always remember this moment. Bruce was kind enough to send Brent a copy of his publicity photo on which he mentions us as being a big influence on his music career. It doesn't get much better than that.

As mentioned earlier, Clifford Curry and Rufus Thomas were both friends and fans of the band. The Tams were fellow artists at Lowery and friends as well. We played many shows together.

As far as honors go, we are recognized by the Georgia Music Hall of Fame in Macon, Georgia. We are represented by a display in the museum. We are in the South Carolina Beach Music Hall of Fame. We are even in the Smithsonian Museum in Washington, DC.

From Left to Right: Bruce Springstein, Jimmy Perkins, Grainger Hines, Shawn McElrath and Brent Fortson.
Medallions on stage perform Double Shot with Bruce.

We received the key to the city in both Greenwood and Ninety Six, South Carolina. Numerous towns across the South have proclaimed Swingin' Medallion Day at some point in time. We have proclamations for both forty-year and fifty-year anniversaries of "Double Shot."

John became good friends with Curtis Mayfield of the Impressions. We performed several times with Maurice Williams and the Zodiacs. We did shows with Bill Pinkney and the Drifters, the Tams and many, many more.

"Double Shot" has sold over a million copies. As previously mentioned, it never reached number one on the charts because of how it was released regionally. It did stay on the charts for twenty-three weeks.

Royalties are paid based on record sales and air-time on all radio stations. A lawyer years later investigated unpaid royalties to various groups. He did the research on our records and collected additional royalties for us. This was a pleasant surprise. The money came from Bill Lowery Talent. Thanks for the bonus! Groups don't make a lot of money from royalties. Most of the money is made by the increase in the amount you charge for an appearance.

I may have overlooked some, but if I have, I apologize. To me, the biggest honor of all is the loyalty of our fans that has lasted over fifty years.

CHAPTER 26

Chicken Man

IT'S TIME TO indulge in a little humor. Most of us had nicknames. John's nickname was Knobs because he was constantly tuning and adjusting all of our equipment. Joe's nickname was Mole because he slept most of the day and stayed up at night. Charlie gave Jimbo his nickname: Mr. Dynamite with a Two-Inch Fuse. Mine was originally Red Man due to my red hair, but it soon became Chicken Man. I loved fried chicken. I guess it's a Southern thing. I nearly always ordered chicken whenever we stopped to eat. They were relentless in teasing me about it.

But there was another much more famous Chicken Man: a radio show we would listen to when traveling late at night. It would always begin with a rooster crowing, followed by a humorous story about the daily adventures of Chicken Man.

We were traveling the back roads of Alabama one night. John and I were in the front seat and Joe was asleep in the back seat. The rooster crowed, and on the radio came Chicken Man. At the same time, a group of real chickens decided to cross the road. Big mistake! We hit several of them, and feathers flew everywhere. John and I hollered. Joe jumped up from the back seat and yelled "What is all this chicken shit? I'm trying to sleep!" John and I laughed all the way to Greenwood.

A 'DOUBLE SHOT' OF LOVE

Swingin' Medallions honored at opening of Uptown Live

Beach music inspired jams once again flooded Uptown on Thursday as the Swingin' Medallions took to the stage at Countybank Plaza to kickoff Uptown Live for the season. Current and original members rocked the crowd that filled the plaza with covers and original tunes, all leading up to the finale, where band members crowded onto the stage to dance along with "Double Shot (Of My Baby's Love)." The 1966 hit song turned 50 years old this year, an event which was commemorated by Mayor Welborn Adams, who issued a proclamation declaring Thursday "Double Shot Day." The young and young at heart spent the night dancing, with fun for all paired with heartfelt tributes to recently lost bandmates — including Hack Bartley. His son, Jake, played alongside founding members through classics and cover songs alike — from Sly and the Family Stone to Lynyrd Skynyrd and plenty in between. More photos of the event along with video of the concert can be found at **indexjournal.com**.

DOWNTOWN ALIVE EVENT IN GREENWOOD, S.C. HONORING THE 50 YEAR ANNIVERSARY OF DOUBLE SHOT.

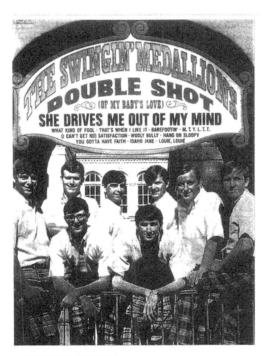

The Party on the Mountain
Celebrating 50 years. Everyone that attended got an 8 X 10 color photo of our album cover.

CHAPTER 27

Memories

IT'S AMAZING HOW many people have a special memory relating to "Double Shot" and the Swingin' Medallions over the years. Here are a few of those:

One night in the 1980s, I got a phone call at home from a deejay at WNOX radio in Knoxville, Tennessee. He wanted to do an interview to tape and play on his oldies show. At the time he called, we were under a tornado warning in Greenwood. We managed to get through the interview, however. We played at the University of Tennessee and in the Knoxville area many times, and he had attended several of those shows. He just wanted to check in and see how we were doing and what we were up to. *Nice!*

The Medallions played in Clinton, South Carolina, in September of 2017, and I was able to attend and join in with them. During an intermission break a man came up to me and asked if I would come speak to his wife, explaining that she was not very mobile. This was an outdoor concert, so I waded through all the lawn chairs to where she was seated in a wheelchair.

She said that she lost both of her parents at a young age. As a result, she was raised in a very strict Baptist orphanage: no dancing and no rock 'n' roll music. Her boyfriend bought her a small transistor radio. (Remember those?) She kept it hidden under her pillow. He would call the local radio stations and request "Double Shot" for her at night. *Wow!* was all I could say.

I received an email recently from a lady who looked me up on the internet. We did a concert in 1965 at an armory in Savannah, Georgia. She said that she was a tall young girl standing against the wall, taking wet paper towels to us to cool off.

She also attended several concerts in Jacksonville Beach, Florida, in 1967–68. She said that she finally mustered up enough courage to come say hi. She just wanted to say hello and added that we were a significant memory in her growing-up years, even from the sidelines. She signed the email saying "a Double Shot fan forever."

I performed with the group on New Year's Eve, 2017, in Newberry, South Carolina, at the Oprah House. This young lady drove by herself from Atlanta, Georgia, to be there. It was great to see her after all these years. Today she is a flight attendant out of Atlanta. She mentioned that on a flight from Baton Rouge, Louisiana, to Atlanta she was walking through the first class section humming "Double Shot" as she walked. A passenger stopped her, said that he recognized the song, and that he used to work for Cyril Fitter who co-wrote "Double Shot" and a couple of songs for the Tams. To use her words: "It's a small world."

In September 2016, we played for Downtown Alive in Greenwood. Joe, Brent, and I made the trip. A large group of my former algebra students was in attendance. They all came up to me to say thanks for being their algebra teacher. We took pictures, chatted about old times, and I even signed a couple of autographs. Can you imagine being thirteen or fourteen years old and having a music celebrity for a teacher?

One of my former students, Dr. Grover Henderson, was a dermatologist in Greenwood. He gave a speech one day at Ninety Six High School. During his speech he mentioned that the best teacher that he ever had was Mr. Carroll Bledsoe for algebra. Little did he know that my granddaughter, Emily Bledsoe, was in attendance. She nearly fainted, but she was very proud to hear those words.

Another memory relates to a time we played a benefit concert for Danny Thomas and St. Jude's hospital in Memphis, Tennessee. We met Danny and his daughter, Marlo Thomas. We had our picture taken with Danny, but we never received a copy.

By far the best part of the whole experience was visiting the hospital and meeting the kids. The hospital is still doing wonderful work and research, and Marlo is carrying on her father's noble work. Above all, the kids are the real warriors and heroes of this story.

The band did a show for the Greenville shag club in 2017 in an airplane hanger at the Greenville downtown airport. The place was packed. A lady came up to me and said thank you. She said that they had set a goal, and, thanks to us, they had made three times the amount of money that they had set for their goal.

Many local musicians in our area have been inspired and assisted by the Swingin' Medallions. John McElrath and his two sons, Shawn and Shane, have been the backbone of this project. They have offered the use of their recording studios, and helped them get bookings and to progress in their careers. Several have gone on to become members of the Swingin' Medallions.

John Scott, a friend of mine from Greenwood, and his wife had dinner with T. Graham Brown and his wife one evening a while back. T. Graham is a country music star and several years ago did a show in Greenwood. When he found out that John was from Greenwood, he asked about the Medallions and how were they doing. John explained that he and I were friends and had worked together years ago. We also raced go carts together.

There have been many, many similar experiences. Every time the band performs somewhere, someone will come up with a new story about a special memory they have of the band. "Do you remember playing my senior prom?" "I remember seeing you in Panama City." "I know all of the moves to the 'Double Shot' dance."

It's stories like these that make it all worthwhile. At the time, you have no idea of the impressions or influences you can have on people. When you hear their stories and memories, it can be most humbling.

CHAPTER 28

In Loving Memory

OVER THE FIFTY-PLUS years of the band, many members have come and gone. Some, like myself, have semi-retired, some have fully retired, and sadly, some have passed away. We have already talked about the tragic death of our young guitar player, David Easter.

Of the original eight members, two have passed away. Charlie Webber died from cancer. Charlie went into law enforcement after leaving the band. He eventually joined SLED (State Law Enforcement Division) for South Carolina. He moved up through the ranks and became a lieutenant. Knowing Charlie, it may have been a general! Charlie went to Clemson University on a full football scholarship, but he had to drop football after his freshman year. They discovered that he was completely blind in one eye. In those days, freshman could not play for the varsity team. Charlie was the starting running back on the freshman squad. His claim to fame was scoring a touchdown against arch rival South Carolina. He dove into the end zone from the one yard line, landed in the T of the word *IPTAY* (in Clemson's logo), and got a mouthful of chalk.

Steve Caldwell also died from cancer. After leaving the music business, Steve moved to Atlanta. There he and his brother, Sonny Caldwell, went into business together. They formed a successful temporary employment agency.

Joe Morris left the group to join the business world. He went to law school and worked with State Farm Insurance. He wound up with Sonoco Packaging Co. On a second round with Sonoco, he was hired to head up their plastic bag division—yes, those grocery store bags. He then started his own company in Mexico and the Caribbean called Packaging Systems International. Joe now lives in Columbia, South Carolina.

Brent Fortson has become a successful lawyer and has his own law firm in Greenville, South Carolina. Brent is like I am: He still enjoys playing and performing and shows up whenever the band is close by.

Jimbo Doares left the band to go into the business world. Jimbo went to work for Monsanto Corporation in Greenwood in their accounting department. He left there years later to go to work for an insurance broker in Greenwood. He and his wife, Amy, live in Greenwood, and he is now retired.

Jimmy Perkins left the group in 1967. He moved to Atlanta, Georgia. He stayed in the music business and played with several successful bands in the Atlanta market. He has now moved back to Greenwood and is once again performing full time with the band.

John McElrath stayed with the band full time. A few years ago, he was diagnosed with Parkinson's disease. He lost his beautiful wife, Jayne, to cancer. His two sons, Shawn and Shane, now carry on his tradition. He has bravely and relentlessly battled this disease. He rarely makes a performance these days, but he continues to offer wisdom, advice, and a lifetime of experience to the band.

I left the group in 1973. As I mentioned earlier, my wife's death forced me off the road. I had some girls to raise. My youngest daughter, Wendy, was just a baby when her mother passed away. My brother, David, and his wife, Joyce, took Wendy home with them to care for her. After much thought and a lot of prayers, we decided that they would adopt her and raise her as their own. This was definitely the hardest decision I have had to make in my life. They did a wonderful job, and I could not be prouder of her or of them. She and her husband both have successful business careers and two wonderful sons. Kelly and Cindy, the two older girls, were raised by me, my mother, and Melody's mother.

I went to work for Child's Furniture Company in Greenwood, South Carolina. Don Childs and I went to high school together. He taught me all about the sales business. While working at Childs, I met my second wife, Gail Bryant. She had two sons from a previous marriage. We had our own version of the Brady Bunch. Sadly, Gail passed away in April, 2012.

Ricky has one daughter, Emily. Scott has a son, Evan, and a daughter, Meredith. Cindy has a daughter, April, and a son, Drake. Kelly has two daughters, Melody and Kai. If you are keeping score that makes seven grandchildren. Ricky and his wife, Kristi, live in Ninety Six. Scott and his wife Lisa live in Greenwood. Cindy and her kids live in St. Simons Island, Georgia. Kelly and her husband Tim live in Carmichael, California.

Over the years several other members have passed away. Gerald Polk from Walterboro, South Carolina died. I still hear from his son on Facebook from time to time. Gerald was a great guy, and we miss him.

Next was Johnny Cox from Enoree, South Carolina. I was able to attend his funeral in Woodruff, South Carolina. Johnny was one of the best all-around musicians to ever play in the band. His father, Paul Cox, is also gone. Johnny and Paul invited me to join their band, the Barrons, while I worked at Childs Furniture. We played only on weekends. We played regularly at the Officers Club at Fort Jackson in Columbia, the Shrine Club in Spartanburg, South Carolina, and the Francis Marion Hotel in Charleston, South Carolina, each New Year's Eve. This kept me in touch with the music world.

Most recently we lost Hack Bartley. Hack died doing something that he loved—fishing. His body was found in a pond where he had gone fishing by himself. No one knows exactly what happened. I feel for his wife Libby and his son Jake. Hack was a great performer and a great showman. A large, sad crowd attended his funeral. Hack formed his own band, Hack Bartley and Shuffle, and Jake played with him. He won several beach music awards for his song "Don't Wait Up for the Shrimp Boats, Mama, Daddy's Coming Home with the Crabs." Hack knew everyone in town, and he will be greatly missed.

We also lost our old buddy, Gary "Cubby" Culbertson to cancer. Cubby lived in Fountain Inn, South Carolina. We met for lunch at the Cracker Barrel restaurant in Greenville shortly before his passing. If it had not been for Cubby there would have been no "Double Shot" for the Medallions.

I miss them all every day. It doesn't seem possible that they are all gone. I will forever cherish the memories of both good and bad times that we went through together.

The Party on the Mountain

2 DeeJays and 5 Medallions

Left to right: Larry Roak, Joey Roberts, Freddy Pugh, Dave Roddy, Carroll Bledsoe, Brent Fortson and Jimmy Perkins

CHAPTER 29

The Party on the Mountain—Fifty Years!

MY FINANCÉE, JENNEANE Froman, and her family put on a Fiftieth Anniversary of Double Shot party on November 29, 2016. It was held at the Party and Event Center in Saluda, North Carolina. There was no cover charge, and admission was by invitation only. We also invited several area shag clubs and even had one club represented from Tennessee. Over five hundred people attended. Former Medallions Freddie Pugh, Perrin Gleaton, Brent Fortson, and I performed with the group.

Pat Patterson and his wife, Robin, came up from Clinton, South Carolina. Pat is a former musician, a deejay, and now owns AM and FM radio stations in Clinton that also air in the Lexington and Columbia markets. Pat played drums and was in several groups over the years—Hack Bartley and Vision, Southern Comfort with Rhonda McDaniel, Fresh Air, and others.

Pat is also on the internet twenty-four hours a day with "Beach, Boogie, Blues and Beyond." You can find it at Largetime.net. Pat does a live show Monday through Friday from 4:00 p.m. until 7:00 p.m., and he loves to take requests. Patman and Robin also have CDs available, and he includes at least one Medallions song on each CD that he produces. Pat and Robin have been longtime supporters of the band, and I am proud to call them my friends. At their home studio in Clinton, they have a wall dedicated to the Medallions. Robin's mother was one of my former students. She was in my homeroom class, so I did not have a chance to ruin her math career.

Dave Ruddle, aka Rockin' Dave Roddy, came up and brought one of his deejay buddies from WSGN radio in Birmingham. If it were not for folks like them, we would not be having this conversation.

We presented each of them with a framed copy of Greenwood's proclamation of "Double Shot's" fiftieth anniversary. We also gave one to each of the band members, both new and old.

This was the party of all parties. People came from Tennessee, Alabama, Georgia, Florida, and of course from North and South Carolina. Everyone in attendance received a full color 8x10" photograph of our album cover. We were glad to autograph many of them. The Medallions sold out of CDs and sold a lot of T-shirts.

Beach music has been best described as *happy music*. There were certainly a lot of happy people on the dance floor that night. Can you say sixtieth year reunion?

This is a photo of the Swingin' Medallions today.
From Left to Right: Jimmy Perkins, Shane McElrath, Larry Freeland, Josh Snelling, John Smith Buchan, Shawn McElrath, Paul Perkins, Chris Crowe, and Larry Roark.

CHAPTER 30

Still Swingin'

THE BAND IS still swinging today as strong as ever. John's two sons, Shawn and Shane, are both in the band. Shawn heads up the group, and Robby Cox, a longtime drummer with the band, handles most the bookings and the business end of the group. Robby now lives in Nashville, Tennessee.

The current band consists of:

Chris Crowe—saxophone, drums, and vocals

Chris is originally from Easley, South Carolina. He owns his own woodworking shop in Greenwood. He is an excellent craftsman in refinishing and repairing furniture. He has done several jobs for us, and I could not be happier with the results of each one of these projects. Chris has been with the group for eight years. He has a music degree from Lander University, is married, and has three children.

John Smith Buchan—trumpet, trombone, and vocals

John Smith was born in Florence, South Carolina, then moved to Anderson, South Carolina. He now lives in Greenwood. He has a wide vocal range and does a bang-up job on falsetto vocals. He went to Clemson University. He played in a couple of bands before coming to Greenwood. He has been with the Medallions for six years.

Josh Snelling—trumpet and vocals

Josh has been in the band for eleven years. He is married and has one son. Josh attends Piedmont Tech and Lander University, both located in Greenwood. He is a talented musician and vocalist.

Jimmy Perkins—saxophone, bass guitar, and vocals

Jimmy lives on Lake Greenwood. He is one of the original members of the band. He left the group in late 1966 after our tour was over and moved to Atlanta. He played with several groups in the Atlanta area before finally moving back to Greenwood. He has now rejoined the band on a full-time basis. He has been back for about three years.

Paul Perkins—drums, vocals, and a great showman

Paul is married and has been with the band for three years. His version of "Just a Gigolo" is a showstopper everywhere the band goes. Paul played with a band called Slewfoot, the band who replaced Alabama at the Bowery in Myrtle Beach, South Carolina. Paul moved to the outer banks of North Carolina before returning home to Greenwood. Slewfoot recorded a couple of country records. He also played with Kinfolk, a popular local band there in Greenwood. Paul is Jimmy's little brother.

Larry Freeland—guitar and vocals

Larry is originally from Plum Branch, South Carolina, in McCormick County. Larry is married, and he and his wife Linda have four children. Larry has been with the band a total of eight years, once for three years and now for five years. He previously played with the Back Water Boogie Band, which later became known as the Back Water Beach Band. They had a record called "Sweet Beach Music" that the Medallions have rerecorded and released. Larry's wife handles the sales of Medallion souvenirs at their shows. Larry also leads two gospel groups: Soul Revival and Praise Time, which keeps him busy.

Larry Roark—keyboard and vocals

Larry has been around since 1962, the very beginning. He has come and gone five times but is now back full time. He also plays in the gospel groups with Larry Freeland and likewise stays very busy. Larry owned a successful heating and cooling business in Ninety Six. He is now retired from that. He took his business location and turned it into a studio where the band now rehearses. His wife, Joyce, and my fiancée have become good friends.

Richard Loper—trumpet and vocals

Richard is from Greenwood and now lives on Lake Greenwood in Laurens County. Richard has been with the band since 1986, thirty-two years off and on. He began with a little group with Shawn and Shane McElrath called the Double Shot Gang. Shawn and Shane told their dad they wanted to be Swingin' Medallions. Richard was internet sales manager at Ballentine Toyota in Greenwood for years. He is now back with the group full time. Richard has one daughter.

Shane McElrath—guitar, saxophone, and vocals

Shane is John's youngest son. He does most of the soul music vocals for the group. Shane started in 1984. He took time off to attend and graduate from the University of Georgia. Shane has been in the group off and on since then.

Shawn McElrath—saxophone, bass guitar, flute, and vocals

Shawn is John's oldest son and a chip off the old block if there ever was one. He has one daughter, Elam, who is good friends and the same age as my granddaughter, Meredith Bledsoe. They played soccer and basketball together at Brewer Middle School in Greenwood. Shawn began playing with the group in 1983. He handles most of the band's day-to-day operations. He does a showstopping version of Junior Walker's hit "Shotgun." He pretends to pass out, then two of the guys pick him up by the legs, hold him upside down, and he continues to play his solo. The crowd always loves it.

Don Reese—sound technician

Don is a retired highway patrolman from the South Carolina Highway Patrol. He handles all of the sound system for the band. All of these adjustments are made with the use of an iPad. He can adjust the overall sound volume and quality as well as each individual microphone and instrument. Modern technology has come a long way from what we had to do in the old days. We did not have microphones on our horns. They have a fantastic sound and plenty of horns. This is still unique in the music world today. They still dance and entertain on stage.

One guiding philosophy of the band has always been: *Have fun!* We knew that if we were enjoying ourselves on stage, that feeling would transfer into the audience. The Medallions truly are the party band of the south. Just like that California deejay said years ago: "Double Shot of My Baby's Love" was a party captured on a record.

Heaven

CHAPTER 31

Post Script

I LOVE BEACH music. I love singing. I try to show up every time the band is playing in the area. I hope that you enjoyed this book as much as I enjoyed writing it. It was great recalling all of these wonderful memories. I hope that it helped call up some good memories for you as well. It was a much simpler time back then than it is today. Jenneane and I now live in Columbus, North Carolina. We are on the very tip top of White Oak Mountain, up 3,250 feet. I wish that everyone could see our little old log cabin in paradise, or as we call it, Heaven.

From the back porch we can see up to seventy-five miles, including Lake Lure and Mt. Mitchell. In the valley below, the color of the fall leaves is spectacular. The snow in the winter is breathtaking.

Y'all come see us sometime! The Swingin' Medallions over the years:

Chris Alexander	Jim Giles	Al Pearson
Eddie Bailey	Perrin Gleaton	Jimmy Perkins
Hack Bartley	Rich Godwin	Paul Perkins
Carroll Bledsoe	Ronnie Goldman	Gerald Polk
John Smith Buchan	Tim Goldman	Fred Pugh
Steve Caldwell	Jimmy Graham	Jimmy Roark
Rich Constant	Johnny Hancock	Larry Roark
Johnny Cox	Irvin Hicks	Robert Sigman
Vanessa Cox	Grainger Hines	Jerry Sims
Robbie Cox	Grey Hines	Alex Smith
Scott Cox	Michael Huey	Howard Smith

Richard Crocker	Chip Jennison	Josh Snelling
Bobby Crowder	Monty Johnston	Taylor Stokes
Cubbie Culbertson	Cambell Josh	Ashley Stokes
Jim Doars	Marvin Koerber	Ronnie Stone
David Eastler	Richard Loper	Dwight Styron
Steve Eddy	Jayne McElrath	Bobby Taylor
Gary Elrod	John McElrath	Kos Weaver
John English	Shane McElrath	Charlie Webber
Brent Fortson	Shawn McElrath	Dale Williams
Wayne Free	Joe Morris	
Larry Freeland	Ron Nobles	

PHOTO GALLERY

Swinging Medallions honored

STAFF REPORT

GREENWOOD - Fifty years ago, a band out of Greenwood recorded a song that would stand the test of time.

The Swinging Medallions, a Southern party band, recorded Double Shot of My Baby's Love. The song would shoot of the charts and made it to No. 17 on Billboards top 100 in 1966.

Monday, band members past and present gathered in Greenwood where Mayor Welborn Adams read a city resolution extolling the band, its origin and longevity.

Four of the original band members, Brent Forston, Carroll Bledsoe, Jimmy Perkins and Joe Morris, joined with younger members to sing the song again.

Another big party is planned for the band and the song on Nov. 19th in Saluda, North Carolina.

PAUL BROWN
The Swinging Medallions performed in Greenwood on Monday night.

10A ‖ THURSDAY, 09.08.16 ‖ GREENVILLEONLINE.COM

ACKNOWLEDGMENTS

MY THANKS GO out to all those who helped in writing this book. I hope that I don't leave anybody out.

- Brent Fortson
- Jimbo Doares
- Joe Morris
- Fred Pugh
- Larry Roark
- Greg Haynes
- Jimmy Perkins
- Chris Crowe
- John McElrath
- Richard Loper
- Dave Ruddle
- Paul Perkins
- Pat Patterson
- John Smith Buckan
- Shane McElrath
- Josh Snelling
- Shawn McElrath
- Larry Freeland